Blessings
Marsha

To Jason,
Best Wishes!
Ed

8/13/13

TRUE HAUNTING
2

By Edwin F. Becker

Dedication

This is dedicated to my wife, Marsha L. Becker and to my daughter, Katherine L. Higdon, who make all things possible for me and to the many readers of True Haunting that relentlessly demanded more.

True Haunting 2

ISBN: 9781943612666

Books by Edwin F. Becker

True Haunting

Banished

Famished

DeathWalker

DeathWalker II

13 Chilling Tales

A Trip Back In Time

Death List

Visit the author at www.EdwinBecker.com

A Note from the Author

It is advised that the reader first reads, **True Haunting**, as this was written assuming the reader has knowledge of the basic story. In writing this, I had a difficult decision. Many people advised me to incorporate all this new material into the original book and republish a new version of True Haunting. I felt this was not fair to the tens of thousands of readers that bought the original book and would have to repurchase it, likely at a higher price being a larger book. Although I hate sequels, especially in nonfiction, I will call this book a companion. Why the second book? In many cases an author shudders when a subject in one of his books surfaces because there is always the possibility that this person or persons disagree with what was written. In my case, it was the opposite. Despite my efforts in trying to locate my tenants, I failed. Instead, after True Haunting was released, one of my tenants emerged from the pages and not only endorsed the book, they revealed many compelling and frightening occurrences of which we were totally unaware.

Then, there was my wife, Marsha. In my youth, I never wanted to know what went on when I was at work. I never asked and avoided listening. Why? Because, I felt helpless in doing anything about it, and guilty that I had to leave her alone and unprotected. In this book, for the first time I interview Marsha and feel some of her fears. How did she cope being there 24/7?

Lastly, is the story of my final tenant Mrs. Scott. It is one that is bizarre and was intentionally left out of the first book, for at that time I felt it didn't add much to the story. Not knowing what happened to our first tenants, I did not see the common thread that seemed to attack and affect every woman that resided on that first floor. So the strange behavior of Mrs. Scott is now revealed. Could there be a True Haunting 3? Who knows? If my other tenants ever surface, or I am able to locate the man to whom I gave the building, it is quite possible. Maybe then I will rewrite to whole book? This historical event that caused paranormal to step into main stream media should be told completely. I feel it is a responsibility. These things are not to be taken lightly or toyed with. If I asked you to come with me to a zoo where ALL the animals ran loose, you would likely refuse and wish me luck. Yet, staying the night in a haunted hotel, or buying tickets to tour a haunted location is considered a common thrill. It baffles me why people will pay for the threat of bringing something home that they never counted on.

Edwin F. Becker, 2015

Introduction

True Haunting was the book that was not supposed to be. It was the story of a very haunted house that was long before Hollywood created the horrific images that have become so very popular. It was Marsha's and my story, and one never intended to be public. I never imagined it would dominate parapsychology in the U.S., and command number one in the U.K. and Canada. This self published unknown author does no advertising or book signings, so the kind words of my readers created a virus that has traveled worldwide. What I never realized was that our experience was significant and historical, and that television never before took notice of anything paranormal. It truly is the first paranormal event that had national TV coverage.

When the book was released, it actually took over the existing paranormal world and altered the perspective of true paranormal activity. No, there was no blood dripping down the walls or flying pig heads, and it caused many people to reevaluate what was being presented as the truth.

A true haunting experience is not frightening from a 'horror' perspective. It, instead, drains your energy, makes you paranoid, affects your health, and causes you to doubt and question your sanity. It is not as scary as it is emotional. Therefore, I know a haunted survivor when I meet one. I can simply see it in their eyes. There isn't excitement in their voice, or laughter or giggles; only serious and sometimes sad moments of recall. There is a PTSD that goes along with these experiences, but most of us find that the telling and retelling of our experience acts much like therapy, in that the more we talk about it, the easier it becomes.

I guess I am a great example, for appearing in SYFY's Paranormal Witness, was actually the very first time we spoke in public. During the filming, the director had to stop three times because my emotions surfaced. After that, I became a sought after radio guest but refused for quite a long time, because of the fear of ridicule, which was left over from the 70's, and my possible inability to answer certain sensitive questions. In the end, I found that the radio hosts were kind and telling my story became therapeutic.

Marsha and I both have a sound paranormal education which is not from the movies for we are not 'horror' fans and are not subscribers of cable, as we only have plain old free television. We do not understand all the technical gizmos people are using, nor do we understand all the various acronyms assigned to certain phenomena. In fact, except for those that are helping people who are affected by these things, we do not understand why someone would chase after something they really do not wish to catch.

Between the book and our Paranormal Witness appearance, it brought us emails and messages from all over the world. It has allowed us to help many people and refer others to experts who are willing to do what we are not capable of. Unlike what we faced in 1970, today, there is help available worldwide.

This was a strange book for me to write, because I chose to write it in my wife, Marsha's voice. I also chose to allow it to be her unaltered memories, as best she can recall, 45 years later. This may not agree at times with the timelines in True Haunting, but there were never any disagreements with the events that took place. It was strange sitting down with my wife of 48 years and finally asking her what went on when I was at work? Most honestly, this was something I had avoided, because as a young man, I could not cope with the fact that I had to go to work and leave her and my baby in that building, vulnerable and sensitive to that unpredictable activity.

Then, there is Dave (real name Dan), who appeared with us in the Paranormal Witness episode. We spent days together and even more hours on the phone, plus he gave me a write up that detailed so many, many things that we were never aware of. This literally affected us in a number of ways. First, we learned that so much went on, as far as paranormal activity that we were completely blind to. Second, was the stress and emotional problems they suffered, and third, was our overall ignorance that a native Mohawk Canadian had much more knowledge and understanding of the spirit world than we did. We felt stupid that we considered Dave 'superstitious,' and hid things from him, when he actually had less fear and more understanding than any of us. I found his lack of fear and acceptance unbelievable, and had to verify this with a few Native American sources. Today, I fully understand why there are few Native American ghost chasers. They are taught about these things and accept them from a very early age. They understand that these things exist and respect this dimension that they cannot control.

So what was the effect on Marsha and me? Releasing True Haunting quickly thrust us into a very large and warm paranormal community. Given our scars of ridicule and skepticism, it was a pleasant relief. One thing that we saw clearly was that today the paranormal world is fragmented. There is a portion dedicated to pure entertainment. This can include TV shows, movies, books, and psychic feats. It seems they have no boundaries for sensationalizing any aspect of the paranormal. With this, the sad part is that sometimes people take it seriously. It seems certain individuals work very hard at attempting to provide and maintain the 'BOO' factor.

One area that we fully support and admire is the many groups that provide various levels of assistance. There are investigators that confirm activity and attempt to expand the scientific knowledge, and healers of all types that will attempt to cleanse spirits from residences and even guide them toward the light. Finally, there are the many exorcists that, with faith and courage, are willing to go head to head with demonic entities that nightmares are made of. This is a very special group.

Marsha and I are a bit removed from the modern paranormal movement. We heard ghosts without any special equipment. We saw a solid apparition and, other than knowing what it was, it was not a horrific image, and was rather ordinary. We have seen objects propelled, so hearing EVP's, or seeing shadows, or seeing a lamp shade wobble, is no big deal. We know what these things can do if they build up enough energy, and always wonder why people are looking for this experience. I personally don't think it can be had unless one decides to take residence and allow the spirits to work their subtle magic and build energy over time.

The one thing that makes me sad is that nothing more is known about these things than what was known 50 years ago. Is there anyone that thinks any of this entertainment is educational? Has this multi-million dollar market of meters and gadgets actually taught us anything? It has taught me quite a lot.

People are easily willing to explore things that can be very dangerous and affect their lives and their families lives...if they can't see it. You cannot cross into that dimension without some amount of residue staying with you. There is not enough caution and respect given to the paranormal. I know, because as a young man, that became my weakness. I had no fear of the invisible, even if it could vibrate a door and move a mixer. In fact, I became angry at being unable to confront these things, and it took my anger and made it a constant part of my personality. I began facing everything in my life with a hostility that I never recognized had overtaken me.

Are we experts? NO! There are no experts that I have ever met or even heard of. There are a few people that have crowned themselves with impressive titles, but only for the sake of obtaining recognition in the media. There is a whole world of dark arts that I never wish to encounter that can conjure other types of undefined energies. Stay away.

Just know that the paranormal is also somewhat undefined. Thus, it is exploited. No, there is no blood dripping down walls. No, there are no dolls running around like Chucky. No, pigs can't fly, and the only flying monkeys are in The Wizard Of OZ. Marsha and I love studying the paranormal, but we will never seek any first hand experiences. Been there...did that. Just know that because these things are invisible, it does not make them any less dangerous.

In this book you will learn of Dave's experience as our tenant. I apologize up front, for the redundant phrases such as, "we had no idea." Learning his story 43 years later was overwhelming and shocking. You will learn about how Marsha coped, and her perspective from the beginning to the end of our ordeal. You will also read of the weird behavior of our final first floor tenant, Mrs. Scott. I hope all of you readers enjoy this book...we didn't!

Edwin F. Becker

CHAPTER ONE

Marsha Finally Speaks

"Unwrapping my present"

What could go wrong? We were both employed, living in a great apartment, and expecting our first child...and then the roof caved in, as our landlady literally told us to get out! She wanted no children. We were in shock, as we had never had a problem renting anything; we were the ideal couple, both working, and the landlords typically had no problem with our cat, for it was dogs that messed up their lawns. Now, with an infant on the way, we hit the wall of discrimination head on. Place after place turned us away. Understand that this was the age of discrimination, and tenants did not have any rights. It wasn't uncommon for landlords to disallow children then, as it is for them to disallow pets now.

It was Ed's birthday, but he insisted that he was going to look at a property that was for sale. He explained it was a situation where the heirs were liquidating a piece of real estate, and that we could possibly work out a way to buy it. He knew that if it was advertised as an 'heir estate,' that it was likely a death in the family that caused the liquidation. In a city of millions, this was all too common. I was a bit surprised at his optimism, as we had very little money saved and our first baby was on the way. We had no insurance, and I knew our obstetrician had to be paid in full as would the hospital...so where would the down payment come from? I never asked, and I relied on him to come up with that answer. Whatever we would do would be our responsibility, because I was not in good standing with my family as far as borrowing and his family was dirt poor. Any loans were out of the question.

Remember, this was the age before credit cards and cash machines. Banks didn't even have branches, as all account records were kept manually on hand written cards. People ask why didn't I go along to see the building? The answer is simple. It was because I was very pregnant and still working. I was exhausted! Plus, it was a man's world, and no written commitment was necessary from a wife. A woman's signature was near-worthless, for financial purposes. Ed knew Chicago like the back of his hand, so I had complete trust in his judgment. I had seen some of the Chicago apartment buildings, and I so hoped it would be one of the stately gray granites that I found so charming, but I was willing to settle for any roof over our heads at this point.

It was late in the afternoon when Ed returned. He announced as positively as he could that we had bought a building. Despite the fact that we had the comfort of knowing there would be a place of our own, I sensed an air of apprehension. This seemed miraculous, since we were really desperate to have someplace to call 'home' when our baby was born. I never asked, and I assumed Ed's apprehension had to do with the responsibility of having a large mortgage and had signed on for 30 years of debt.

Ed made it very clear that the property was not in the best condition and he seemed to overemphasize that fact. My hopes fell as I learned it was not my stately gray granite. We were currently living at the edge of Chicago, only blocks from the suburb of Niles, and in a very nice residential neighborhood. He explained that we would be moving to the near-north side and although 'safe,' it was not as appealing as where we were now.

As best as he could, he described the two story building and the fact that we could rent the one apartment to help pay the mortgage, which would be a bit of an offset to me not working. He talked of the area being more congested, racially mixed, and there would not be any end to the work we would have to do to put the building in shape. In summary, I found it unusual that although I haven't even seen it yet, he was already assuring me we would be moving out before our expected baby went to preschool. I knew for sure that he certainly did not purchase the house of his dreams if his plan to move out was already on his mind before we even moved in.

He told me we could tour the property the next coming Saturday. In a way, it was like waiting to unwrap a present and it seemed to be the longest week ever. Ed never realized how much he talked about fixing the place up. It was as if he was preparing me to lower my expectations. I was still working and he also had to work a half-day on Saturday, so it was around 1 PM when we began our journey. I was not that familiar with Chicago, so I watched as the buildings went from houses, to two and three story apartment buildings, and began getting older and older. It was only years later that Ed told me his drive was strategic, as he took the nicest and most scenic route; avoiding some of the deteriorating neighborhoods. I remember a beautiful old church when Ed turned the corner and began driving down the street. I immediately noticed that as far as I could see was a street lined with apartment buildings that had an obvious parking problem, as there were more apartments than places to park.

Even though we took the closest parking spot that was open and not directly in front of the building, I knew which building it was. This building stood out like a sore thumb. The wrapping paper came off the present and my excitement evaporated. Ed never had to point it out, as it was the worst looking building on the block. True, it was in need of repair and paint, but that was not the issue. For me, there was a dark cloud hanging over this building. Ed pointed the building out and was studying my expression, so I put on the happiest face I could. I sensed he was becoming serious, and I did not quite understand why, but then, I knew nothing of old Myra. All Ed told me was that a crabby old woman lived on the first floor. He totally left out the part about her being completely insane!

As we crossed the street and approached the building, I did not find the neighborhood as unpleasant and threatening as Ed had described. The buildings were a mixture of frame and brick, and were mostly well kept. There was a huge elm tree near the front of our building and I hoped it was the tree that gave me the impression of a dark shadow. Ed asked me to be quiet as he opened the entrance door. We entered the hallway, turning left toward the stairwell leading to the second floor. In retrospect, I found Ed being quiet and moving silently humorous, because most times he is like a bull in a china closet.

That damned stairwell! Being vacant, there was no electricity to the second floor and the stairwell had a small window near the top, but it faced north and was blocked by the building next door. All we had was a dim glow. This old building with 10 foot ceilings, made this dark stairwell and the number of stairs to the second floor almost appear endless.

It was at this point that I felt uncomfortable. As we walked up the stairwell, there was a landing and a 90 degree turn with a few more stairs ending at the door to the apartment. He unlocked the door and instantly I experienced two overwhelming feelings. One, I strongly felt we were walking into someone else's apartment, and two, the air was thick and heavy. It was not the musty odor that bothered me, but the fact that breathing became more laborious. Though it was a bright sunny day, the apartment seemed darker than it should have been. There was some muted light in the front room because it was lined with windows. The kitchen in the rear was semi-lit, since it also had windows. The enclosed back porch was lined with windows as well.

Ed led the way, but honestly, I heard little of his nervous talk. Instead, I was picturing what we could do with this place. It was littered with furniture. Some of the upholstered furniture had actually been cut open. There was litter about the room; papers, clothes, pots, and pans scattered throughout from front to back. The walls were covered in faded and peeling wallpaper and the floors had worn linoleum. [*linoleum was like vinyl flooring, but made from a tar paper-like material.*] There wasn't a single room that was livable.

I guessed it had been decorated and last cared for decades ago. I hoped the kitchen would be acceptable, but my hopes were dashed when all it contained was a huge homemade combination counter and cabinet, and an old porcelain sink that had legs. I really hoped Ed was prepared for this, because these were the days long before there were home improvement centers. There were no quick fixes.

As Ed led the way out to the enclosed porch, I felt relief for at least the porch was open and bright. Once again, he had us tiptoe down the stairs and out the back porch door. At that time, I never understood why he was being so careful not to disturb this old woman, but soon I would find out first hand. Once outside, he unlocked the door to the basement and began talking about how he would make it into a laundry room for both the apartments. Ed turned around to shush me, as he realized the interior door to the basement from the first floor was off the hinges, and open to old Myra. Therefore she could likely hear us talking. I had yet to realize why he did not want to me to meet her. Ed really shouldn't have had any worries, because I took one step in and I felt so repulsed that I immediately backed out. The basement was dug out and the concrete poured long after the building had been built, but it was not the crudeness that scared me. It was the instant feeling that something there did not want me to enter. It was like if I entered, I would be stepping into another world.

"What's wrong?" Ed asked.

"I am not coming down here." I could see the shock on his face, because I had never before stated anything so emphatically.

"Why?"

"There is just no way I will come down here. I don't like it here."

He pointed toward an old washing machine that had a wringer with rollers attached. "Hey, we have a washer right here!"

I shook my head. "No! I don't care. I won't come down here and won't use that washer!"

He thought it was the basement concept entirely, as I was from Tulsa and having a basement was highly unusual. Going below ground was normally associated with a storm shelter and a tornado. I never saw a true basement before, and Ed thought that was the problem. Of course it wasn't. It was the strong feeling that something in that basement did not want me there. I said nothing, and he was immediately accommodating as he suggested running a gas line to the enclosed porch and putting a dryer just outside the kitchen. I could tell he was confused about my attitude. Ed locked it up and we followed our trail backward up the stairs, through the apartment, and out to the street. Honestly, I didn't know the building was haunted at this point, but I did know I felt feelings I had never felt before, and I was confused by them.

Our whole trip home was spent talking about the possibilities of what we could do with the building. Since it was the first week in August and the closing would be in November, he would ask if he could start fixing up the apartment right away. So when we returned home, he called the real estate company and made that request. Yes, we had to get home to a land line as there were no cell phones in 1970! There were also no area codes and no call waiting. Hold on to your seats, as there was also no answering machines!

All I knew was that a few days later, Ed was on the phone yelling, "Why the hell not? You have nothing to lose. If the mortgage falls through, you get the place decorated and fixed up for free!" I remember laughing as he began to explain to them like he would to someone that was brain dead. "Listen! I will clean and I will paint and if the mortgage is not approved, all my expenses and efforts are yours...for free! Understand? Free! You have nothing to lose!" Eventually, he slammed the phone down.

"These stupid ass people! If we clean the apartment up and decorate and don't get the mortgage, they get what we invested for free. Are they idiots? I told them I would sign off on all liability. It makes no damned sense!"

He was steaming, and it would only be months later that we would learn why they did not want us in the building. It was haunted and they absolutely knew it. But there weren't any disclosure laws in 1970, and any mention of it being a haunted house would only have people questioning one's sanity. As far as I know, we both stayed completely away until the mortgage was approved and a closing date of November 12th was set. Our landlady was fixed on us being out on December 1st, so I knew Ed had his work cut out for him. He would only have from November 13th to November 30th to get all this work done. It sounded impossible. His attitude was for me to simply sit back and have our baby! So, aside from having financial problems, we were on top of the world. We would soon be parents and living in a building we owned. I worked until my 9th month and after that, our income dropped by half. The immediate problems we faced were all financial. I cannot even describe how many days we ate Ragu and shells, stretching a pound of hamburger across three meals. During this time, I swear, McDonald's would have been a great treat, as we saved every cent.

When the obstetrician mailed us his bill, we paid it in full. It was substantial in its day, as it was for the complete pre and post natal care and delivery. After our daughter was born, I spent a total of three days in the hospital. Ed called them to set up a time to pick me up. He was informed that I would not be released until the bill was paid in full. He had the money and it cleaned us out financially, but today we wonder, what if we did not have all the money? Would they have never released me? Would I still be there?

We needed money for the closing and all the materials to fix the place up, so we were really in a tough position. We were now only a month from closing and things looked bleak. Out of the blue came a near-miracle…we thought. Ed received a call from the real estate company and the owners requested that Myra, that old woman, stay 90 to 120 days after the closing. He immediately saw it as an opportunity, and since having Myra leave was his only contingency in the contract he knew he had them over a barrel. Ed asked for Myra's rent to be paid in advance at closing and set the amount as what we likely needed to close. In fact, he would accept their check and use it to pay our closing costs. They quickly agreed, almost within the hour.

It seemed no one in their family wanted Myra, so they needed time to find a place to put her. Although Ed would celebrate this as a victory, it made me wonder if this Myra was more than just a cranky old lady.

It was at the closing that we saw firsthand the hostility and hatred within this family. All I remember is a room full of people representing the heirs, each with their own attorney. There wasn't any social conversation between them and an argument broke out over splitting the cost of the real estate photos. There was no surprise why Myra had nowhere to go. At this point, I felt sorry for the poor old woman, but my sympathy would only last until we had our first clash. Although Ed put the title in both our names, it was he that signed stacks of papers.

Today, with what we have learned about ghosts in the last 40 years, we know Ed declared war with this infestation of ghosts immediately. We were ignorant at the time, but he had made a deal with a second hand store owner to empty the place. He would have the apartment completely emptied of all furniture and minor belongings, so if the ghosts had any attachments to these items, it likely lit a fuse. After the closing, there was no celebration, as Ed left to visit the building and change all the locks. He wanted new locks immediately, because of the hatred we had witnessed and the fact that the second floor apartment had been, in his estimation, vandalized by their own family. So, although he had no electricity turned on yet, he was off to change locks in the dark.

At this point, I was excited, for we had been married over 3 years and I had suffered two miscarriages, so holding our newborn daughter was a feeling I can't even describe. As all new mothers know, I was always exhausted and getting little sleep, but almost immediately I felt I should start packing. Although the uncomfortable feelings about our "new" building stayed with me, I began to think it was all within me and that after we moved in with our things, it would become home. After all, I was used to a newer, cleaner city, primarily comprised of single-family homes, so nearly everything about Chicago made me a bit uncomfortable. During this period, knowing we would be able to collect rent and I could stay home with our baby, was a great feeling to look forward to.

As the weeks went by, I became more excited. Ed would bring samples of the paint, wallpaper, and carpet, and I started to picture the apartment transformed from the disaster I saw into something sparkling and fresh. This may sound as if we had money to decorate, but the truth was that he would get paint from a paint store where people had ordered color mixtures and never picked them up, so the paint was $1 a gallon. The carpeting was all remnants. It was new carpeting, but not wall to wall. The major concerns that he had were just not a factor regarding me not liking the urban area and old buildings, as I actually felt a degree of safety living in an area with a dense population. The old buildings that he thought I would not like were, in fact, charming with interesting architecture and stained glass windows. Sure, our building didn't measure up, but we both had big plans for improvements.

Soon it was moving day. It fell on a weekday and we rented a truck. The only help we could get was from our blind friend, George. I really did not know George that well, but knew he was blinded serving in Viet Nam. I could not see Ed moving everything with only a blind man as a helper, so I was somewhat worried, but from my perspective, the move went rather smooth. As fast as George and Ed unloaded the boxes, I would empty them and set items in the proper rooms where they belonged. It was that very day that I witnessed my first event. I opened a box which held one of my favorite pieces. It was a crystal candy dish, about six inches around. I set it in the center of our living room coffee table. Stepping back, I admired how beautiful it looked. I bent over, pulling out and unwrapping the matching ashtray. When I turned around, the candy dish had moved! It was now teetering on the edge of the table.

I shook my head in wonder as to how it got there. So, again, I moved it to the center and dipped into the box, pulling out another item. Once again, when I turned around, the candy dish had moved. This was not a scary event, but a curious one. I started to think it was me. I was sleep deprived and excited, so perhaps this was just my imagination. I rationalized that either the table was uneven, or the top was too waxed and it was sliding, so I set the dish on one of my grandmother's old doilies. Going about my unpacking, I turned...for a third time and the candy dish had moved...but the doily didn't.

This went by without a mention, but caused me to be vigilant about how and where I put things. I knew what I thought I saw...or did I? That was the beginning of the mind games these things can play. It also led to another event that would become a habit. I shared everything with Ed, but I did not share this. Pretty soon, there were a lot of things I would not share. This was the beginning of Ed and me living in two different worlds. It is one of the things that spirits attempt to do...divide and conquer.

The apartment floor plan was simple. Basically it was three main rooms with a small bedroom adjacent to each. Front to back: Living room, dining room, and kitchen. We designated the front bedroom for the baby, as it had a huge window and was the brightest room. We didn't have any baby furniture yet, except for a dresser bought as a gift from my mom, so she slept in a bassinet beside our bed, which was the second bedroom. I found myself taking the baby and spending the day in the kitchen. It was the only main room that seemed bright, and it had an 'escape' door to the enclosed back porch. So I would either wheel the bassinet into the kitchen, or use what was called a 'baby bouncer.' The bouncer allowed the baby to lie securely, and had a design that allowed you to rock it [bounce it] with your foot. Car seats had yet to be invented.

There were a number of things that I was totally unaware of. Ed had found a storage shed in the basement containing old pornography. He told me they were just old magazines. I knew nothing of the shoe boxes full of magazine cut-out body parts. This may have been another declaration of war with the ghosts, as he eventually sold most everything in that room to a magazine dealer for $60. The dealer did not want the shoe boxes with the cut-outs, so they were left for him to dispose of. All these books had one name on them, and it was Ben.

Ed knew Ben was some kind of deviate, but never shared that with me until a later date. He also had already heard a number of negative things about the family from our next door neighbor, and the owner of the second hand store that took everything from our apartment. So he was building a profile and literally kept everything he learned from me. In fact, I had yet to meet Myra, that lived on our first floor...but that would soon change.

The only issue I had in the first week was that since the baby and I would spend our days in the kitchen, I asked Ed to get me a small portable black & white TV. That first week was fairly quiet, or if anything did happen, I was too busy to notice. I was moving things around and organizing from the closets to the pantry. It was the next week that things began to occur and I began to take notice. When these things happen, unless they are drastic, one typically attributes them to not remembering where you put something, or just accepting that something is not where you thought it was. Certain events just didn't register, as I had an apartment to put in order and a baby to take care of.

We finally had a telephone installed. We had the line installed in the living room, which was strategically placed since we could only afford one phone. In 1970, phones had to be leased and were actually illegal to own... and very expensive. We could only afford one jack, so it was installed in the middle of the apartment so that we could get to the phone equally fast from anywhere in the house. Hearing the ring of the old phones was never a problem, as they were loud and distinctive.

I was not consciously aware that I had made the kitchen my place of choice all day, every day. At first, I never realized that I did not feel comfortable in any other room of the house. Initially, I subconsciously avoided any of the other rooms, including the bathroom. I should have taken notice, because one of my favorite things to do was to lie on the couch and watch our color TV. Instead, I was sitting in a chair, next to the back door, watching a tiny black & white TV, with the baby at my side. The kitchen was to become my fortress.

It was soon after the phone was installed that Ed came home fuming. He was upset, because he had been calling all day from work and all he heard was a busy signal. He went on and on about me being on the phone all day and how expensive that would be. You see, in those days, they charged about 5 cents a minute for local calls. There was no call waiting, no message systems, and not even area codes. Everything was 'operator assisted' with a cost.

He was angry with me and I was completely confused. I responded that I had never touched the phone. I didn't have any friends in Chicago, being from Tulsa, and thus, had no reason to use it. The truth was that, for the most part, I did not even like any of his friends. His musician friends seemed arrogant, looking down at 'day' people, and his childhood friends were of a very rough nature. The women were loud, brash, and looked upon me as a southern church mouse. So, I had no friends. We walked into the front room and there was the phone, completely off the hook. The receiver sat on the table, as if someone had set it down. This made no difference, because now Ed went on about the fact that I should have noticed it.

I had spent my day sitting in kitchen caring for the baby. I even did the laundry in the kitchen, as we had a washer that attached to the sink and my dryer was on the enclosed back porch. I knew Ed didn't believe me, and from festering all day, he gradually calmed down before eating dinner and going downstairs to work on cleaning the basement. That became our routine. He would return home and work for any number of hours, cleaning or painting or fixing the house. The only time we enjoyed was in the early morning. I would wake him up at 5:00 AM, and he would start the water for his bath and we would sit drinking our morning coffee and discuss how and what we might face that day.

I don't remember exactly what day it happened, but I do remember the first occurrence that caught my attention. Christine was napping in her bassinet and I was sitting at the table, quietly watching TV. When I did this, I always sat facing the windows and the back porch, and on my right stood the combination counter and cabinets. I first saw it out of the corner of my eye, but turned to face it head on. The old cabinet door slowly opened. It gave me a chill for no reason other than it opened slowly and deliberately, not like it opened quickly. It opened as if an invisible hand was doing it. I watched as it stayed open. At this point, I just thought it weird.

While still watching my soap opera, I got up and closed the door. Unlike Ed, I was always a believer in ghosts. I wasn't an expert and I hadn't had any ghostly experiences, but I did believe that these things existed. I had visited a "fortune teller" in my late-teens that proved with her accuracy of the telling of my future that these mysterious occurrences can be real. I never knew how these energies manifest, but I knew ghosts exist. The problem with most people who experience this kind of phenomena is that one expects "spooky" things to happen, and not just the simple opening of a cabinet door.

There was no sound, no mist, no fog or anything else; just the slow silent opening of a cabinet door. My reasoning wanted to think the door was faulty in some way, so I would ask Ed to solve it. What I didn't know nor check, was that the phone was also off the hook. Ed came home angry again. It is what these entities do; they get between your relationships. So instead of a kiss, a hug, and some loving words he became instantly hostile.

"I called you all damned day! I suppose you were not on the phone?"

"I never even looked at the phone..."

"I saw it was off the hook, but I suppose you never noticed it."

"I never did."

"Well, maybe our cat was calling her relatives!" Ed was getting sarcastic.

"Funny, but maybe she did knock it off the cradle..." In my mind, it was certainly possible that Kitty knocked it off. What other explanation could there be?

Once again, as Ed changed into work clothes, I prepared for a tense dinner. This became their game. Little things that create a wedge in your relationship and creates negative emotion, which we began feeding them. No one can ever tell me these spirits are not intelligent, as their next move seemed so strategic. There was no doubt that we would look forward to a number of tense evenings; aside from our ghostly occupants, we also had financial problems. There was no rent, as Myra's family had paid us months in advance and we used it up at closing, so we were stretching every penny. However, we still had our coffee and treasured our quiet talks in the morning.

I don't remember the exact day, but it was early one morning when Ed and I finished our coffee and he proceeded to his bath, which was a free standing tub without a shower. All I remember hearing was, "Son-Of-A-Bitch!"

When he entered the bathroom, the tub was empty and the plug and chain were wrapped around the faucet. Our apartment only had an old 30 gallon hot water heater, so his bath was tepid at best. I still remember he rationalized that it was sewer gas that forced the plug out. He thought he just had to cram the plug down a bit tighter. Regardless, he was very unhappy.

The cabinet door became an ongoing event, as at least once a day I would find it, or see it, open. I didn't understand it, because it seemed to close just fine. Our morning time had an ongoing interruption, as Ed started jumping up and checking the bathtub plug. Days went by and Ed patted himself on the back, because jamming the plug down tighter seemed to have solved the problem. Eventually, he stopped checking and no sooner than he did, it began again. Again I would hear, "Son-Of-A-Bitch," as the tub was empty and the hot water had gone down the drain. This routine happened countless times, and soon the ghosts had a victory and destroyed our enjoyable morning coffee and talks, for eventually Ed took his coffee into the bathroom and sat, staring at the plug. Their 'divide and conquer strategy' worked, and we lost that precious morning time that helped us remain close.

We were out shopping and returned home when I had my first introduction to Myra. As we entered the front door, she opened hers and began raving. I was in shock as this dirty, hateful old woman began screaming while clutching a filthy little poodle on her shoulder. I stared in awe and held the baby tightly, as Myra's filthy matted hair was being picked at by the dog and her level of anger was shocking. I watched as Ed's face turned fifty shades of red. All I caught was something like:

"You bastards don't belong here! You sons-a-bitches!"

When she said sons-a-bitches, she spit it out in anger.

This was not the old lady that Ed had described. I instantly knew why we always had to tiptoe past her door. She seemed so angry that I almost thought she would take a swing at Ed with her free hand as she waved it in his face.

"You put a cigarette out in my coffee! You bastards moved my kitchen chairs! Stay out of my apartment, you bastards! We don't want you here!" She shouted.

Ed exploded. "Get back in your apartment or I will kick your ass out! We have no reason to come into your apartment. Now get back in there and shut the hell up!"

"The both of you! You don't belong here! We don't want you here! You sons-a-bitches!" she continued her rant.

"Myra, get back in your apartment and mind your our own business. I swear I will throw your ass out in the street!"

I had never seen Ed talk this way to an old woman, but it seemed to have worked, as she backed away from us and slowly closed the door while glaring all the way.

"I am sorry you had to see that. It was the only way to handle her. I am counting the days until that old witch is gone."

I knew he felt bad and was embarrassed by the encounter. As we walked up the stairs, I kept looking back, expecting her to pop out and continue her tirade. This was a woman one might never forget, as she was not only memorable in appearance, but far from what you would expect from a woman her age. The incident stayed with me for the balance of the day.

Within weeks, our whole lives had changed, along with our personalities. Ed, who was a person that loved to laugh, became serious and irritable, as his personal time that he normally spent playing, or listening to music, was gone. His reading time and love of books was gone, as he worked 10 hour days, quickly ate dinner, and worked 3-5 hours cleaning, painting, or fixing the old house. For a time, I did what I could to not bring up my fears. I loved being a mom, but felt guilty that I was no longer working and helping to relieve our financial woes.

It was weeks later that I mentioned the cabinet door to Ed. I still remember him shaking his head and explaining that the cabinet was likely tilted a few degrees forward, and it was all gravity. He has always been a logical person, so this was the most logical reason for this happening. It was that very logical mind that came between us at times. I remember our discussion, where I tried to explain that it happens almost predictably at the same time most days, and not random. He immediately jumped up and said, "I'll be right back." I wondered where he was going. He returned with a tool called a level. As I watched, he removed all the dishes on the bottom shelf of the cabinet, then he laid his leveling tool on it, and I watched as he shook his head. "Impossible," he stated.

"This cabinet tilts a few degrees inward toward the wall. If that cabinet door opens on its own, this would be defying gravity."

The manner in which he stated this fact implied that I might be imagining this happening.

"I don't know about gravity, but I do know it opens and stays open almost every afternoon," I replied.

"Well, I have never seen it open on its own and since it only happens when I'm at work, likely I never will and if it does, so what? Just close it. If it bothers you that much, I'll put a damn lock on it."

That was Ed. He never wanted to waste his time figuring out why things happen; instead, he created a solution. While others scratched their heads wondering why, only after he fixed things would he try to figure out the cause. I never suggested we had a ghost yet, but I was beginning to become aware that these "little" things were being executed by something we could not see or control.

Ed began finding out that there was not always a solution. It was one night during dinner that the kitchen lights began flickering. It was an on and off pattern and as time went on, we realized it was only during our dinner. Ed checked the wiring and he said it seemed okay, so he decided it must be the light fixture, as it was very old. This resulted in him buying and installing a new one.

I remember him proudly looking up and saying, "That solves that!"

It did until the next evening when his new fixture began the same flickering. He was pissed! He had no remedy for it. Ed had checked the wiring, bought a new fixture, and even installed new bulbs, but the flickering became routine...and happened only in the evenings. It was around this time that I noticed a change in him. He more or less accepted this anomaly, which was not like him at all. He began addressing the event by saying something like, "Okay Ben, have your fun." At this point, I wondered who the hell was Ben?

I was frustrated, because although I never confronted Ed on the subject of ghosts, I knew that even though he denied it, he was accepting the fact that unexplained things were happening. I also wondered, what else was he aware of that he kept from me? He never seemed frightened; in fact, it was the opposite, as he would get angry.

We had set the date to have our daughter Christened. It would be a celebration, as we invited family and friends to join us. Believe it or not, some did not attend because they feared coming to this part of the inner city. In the end, about 14-16 people showed up, and we had set up a buffet. Ed, being Catholic, invited the parish priest, Father Barnes, to join us and bless our home.

There was no 'paranormal' reason for this, only that it was a Catholic tradition. I was raised Baptist and Episcopal, but religion never was a factor in our relationship. Having our daughter baptized Catholic was fine with me, as Jesus Christ was our common denominator. It gave me great comfort that the house was to be blessed. Ed had arranged everything with the church. After the baptism, he would bring Father Barnes to our apartment and he would bless the apartment and join us for lunch.

There wasn't any doubt at this time that we had at least one ghost in this apartment. I imagined it was the man that died there. The fact that a person died prior to us buying the building meant little to Ed. He would eventually explain that this whole neighborhood had buildings that were turn of the century, so every building likely had deaths that occurred within. After all, they once held funerals in the living rooms of these old turn of the century buildings. He grew up in neighborhoods like this and lived in old buildings throughout his childhood.

I have always felt this was the reason he could not interpret the signals they were sending; he had experienced most of these his whole life. The few rooms in our apartment that were noticeably cooler, Ed thought a great benefit, as we wouldn't need an air conditioner. In the summer, it was an advantage, and in the winter, Ed's excuse was that we were distant from the old gas space heater. He rationalized everything, or seemed to come up with a solution to solve, or explain, most activity.

The ghosts began getting more active as time went on. The next event that I remember was the broom. We had a small pantry off the kitchen and there is where I put the broom and dustpan. I am kind of a clean freak, and I would sweep the kitchen floor every day whether it needed it or not. This was another one of those moments when you begin by questioning your own behavior. I don't know when it occurred, but I found the broom leaning against the door outside the pantry. The first time I actually thought I did it without thinking. Then it began happening more frequently. Things were adding up little by little.

People sometimes think these things are not frightening, but they become frightening. It was like they wanted my attention, as the kitchen seemed the center of activity. Looking back, our daughter's room was blessed and never did we have an occurrence or a thing out of place in that room.

There I would be, watching my little TV or feeding the baby, and the cabinet door would slowly open. It was always no surprise that when I went to close it, I would turn around and the broom would be outside of the pantry in the same position. None of this may sound frightening by itself, but it was about this time that I became slightly afraid. I realized they likely could see me and were toying with my reactions, and I had the overwhelming feeling that I was being watched.

I began to wonder, what comes next? I kept the baby near me and always stayed close to that back door. I did not bring up the subject of ghosts to Ed, because I knew what his response might be. He possibly would have installed some kind of lock to hold the broom, or even padlock the whole pantry and in his thinking…that would solve that!

I did make one mistake at this point. I always left the back door unlocked and the screen door had no latch at all. This meant anyone could come barging in and so, I would soon meet Myra face to face!

Chapter Two

What can possibly happen next?

My anxiety was building day by day. Looking back, the spirits were gradually building their energy, separating us emotionally, and we were both changing. That is what these things do. They do not come at you with force; they move in subtly. Unlike what people might imagine, there had yet to be bumps in the night or any real attempts to scare us. Instead, our activity seemed fixated on me during the daytime. I knew Ed had gone beyond his complete disbelief and was likely very aware, but for now he was happy being in a state of denial. We had no knowledge of these things, and his typical solution became to undo whatever they did, or ignore it.

It was clear to me that I was becoming more frightened. At this point, a dish moving, the broom out of place, the cabinet door opening, lights flicking, bath tub unplugged, or the phone coming off the hook, were all becoming routine. What started to eat at me was the question, what comes next? It is at this point that people who endure these things start living in anticipation and walking on egg shells. In a way, I wish a Frankenstein monster came screaming out of the closet, because something like that would have had us sleeping in the car and long gone... but that is not how a True Haunting proceeds.

It was a beautiful morning and the third bedroom was adjacent to the kitchen, which we had made the play room. It contained a baby swing, a playpen, and a pile of stuffed toys. The baby was in her bassinet taking a nap and I had a precious few hours all to myself. I was watching the little TV, immersed in the world of soap operas. I never saw her coming, as Myra opened the screen door and threw the kitchen door wide open. For an instant I was in shock. I only had time for a glimpse before she came barging in. She did not have her dog cradled on her shoulder this time, and she was flailing both arms in the air. Instantly, my mother's instincts kicked in, and I put myself between her and my baby. I am 4'11," and I would have guessed Myra to be about 5' 5." She was screaming at me with her lips tightened, spitting out words.

"You Sons-A-Bitches, you put fucking cigarettes in my coffee! You put your cigarettes out in MY coffee! This is our house and you don't belong here! You and your fucking husband are moving my kitchen chairs! I know what you did! You Sons-A-Bitches!"

It was exactly the same thing she confronted us about the first time I saw her. She looked the same, with the same dress and wild hair sticking out in all directions. I tried to explain and remain calm.

"Myra, I have never been in your apartment. I did not do anything to your coffee!" I responded as calmly as I could, for I was facing what appeared to be someone who was possibly violently insane. I studied her and that house dress looked as if she had been wearing it for a month. Her gray hair was sticking out all over and appeared filthy. Her piercing blue eyes projected pure hatred.

"You lie! You fucking lie! Don't you dare put cigarettes in my coffee ever again! I know you did it! I know you did! Leave us alone!" she screamed.

The baby was now awake and beginning to cry, so as calmly yet as forceful as I could, I looked her in the eyes and demanded, "Myra, you must leave! Go back downstairs to your own apartment. Now!"

For what seemed to be forever, we stood face to face, glaring at each other. With my great relief, she turned, all the while cursing, and walked out, never closing the door behind her. When I went to put the latch on the screen door, I realized it didn't have a latch, so I slammed and locked the kitchen door. Christine was now fully awake and fussing, but I did not pick her up immediately, because I was shaking. It is very difficult for me to describe the force of Myra. From a distance, one might take her as a frail old woman, but in reality, she projected a hatred that made her frightening. I could feel the force when she was in my presence. Just the way she opened and flung the door showed her strength. Looking Myra in the eyes made me feel like a potential victim. Ed underestimated this old woman; this was not your run-of-the-mill cranky old lady that he described, but more of a woman who was insane or possessed. I will always remember that stare of anger and hatred.

I recall picking the baby up and just rocking back and forth nervously. I knew, of course, that we never bothered Myra, but what if she decided that we did? Was I in danger? What was she really capable of? It seemed like much longer, but Ed finally arrived home a few hours later. When I told him what happened, he was more than angry. He had the phone number of the real estate man, and he called and told him to contact the family and warn them that if she were to trespass again, we would call the police and evict her. I began to give Ed hell for not telling me how crazy she was. He explained that the few times he had dealt with her it was more nonsense than anything. He immediately put a latch on the outer screen door so it could be locked. After dinner, he was on the phone to get us a watch dog.

The result was the very next day, we met Holly. Holly was some kind of Alaskan and Shepherd mix, but looked every bit like a wolf. Holly seemed too gentle, as she loved the cat and the baby and was so submissive to both of us, but Ed knew that once she became a member of the family, there was no better protection dog one could get.

I loved Holly, and it was only days later that I heard her roar of a bark. I assumed someone was on the back porch, and Holly was letting me know. She went to the back door and began her warning bark. I was impressed. As if understanding, she began spending her days watching over the baby. I admit, having Holly made me feel much safer, but animals also can put you on alert without making a sound. There were times when I would see her look out into the front room, as her eyes and head seemed to be watching and following something I could not see. I have learned over the years that dogs, cats, and birds can see ghosts at times, and since the majority of ghosts are benign, other than curiosity, most animals won't react. Only when threatened will they act in defense or flee. BUT, this was 1970, and I was not that smart...so I only found her behavior curious.

Maybe it was a reaction to Myra's outburst, or maybe it was a response to the dog being a new strange occupant, but I found out what came next. I went to use the bathroom, and returned to the kitchen. The faucet, an old two handle sink, had been turned on and the cold water was running slowly. I knew immediately that this would add to the list. Now I would have to watch the faucet. Some people may wonder why I stayed in the kitchen with this activity surrounding me. I have no clear answer, other than it was brighter and I had my escape door. I also had this feeling like I was at the mouth of a dark cave, and I did not want to move further in. In the kitchen I could look out the window and cling to the outer world.

Ed and I both looked forward to the Christening and to the building being blessed. When that Sunday finally came, we attended mass and afterward, the Christening. I was not Catholic, but I found being inside this cathedral-like church comforting. When the ceremony ended, I left with family and friends, and Ed waited for the priest. We walked home on this unusually warm winter day and began setting up tables and chairs, preparing the buffet lunch. It was only 20 to 30 minutes, and I heard yelling coming from downstairs. Apparently, Ed and the priest had a confrontation with Myra, but all I heard was Ed, yelling. I had a knot in my stomach as they entered the apartment, both looking serious. I watched as the priest opened his leather case and began what looked to me as preparing for the blessing. I was a bit confused, as we were supposed to have lunch.

As I watched, the priest produced a small manual and a shiny brass object, which I would later learn was a holy water dispenser. He looked toward Ed and stated he would bless the house first. Almost everyone was Catholic, so a reverence came over our guests. The priest walked to the center of the living room and he recited something in Latin and raised his hand, as if he was going to sprinkle holy water. As his hand was raised over his head, the utensil shattered with water and brass falling onto our shag carpet. Unlike in movies, there was no thunderous sound, it just silently crumpled. I, along with everyone else, was stunned. I am positive no one but me had an inkling of what was happening. If anyone did…it was the priest. He crossed himself and bent down and began picking up the pieces. I looked to Ed, who was standing with his mouth open. I knew if we had no audience, he would have said, "WTF?"

Once the priest picked up the pieces, he announced, "I must go." I saw Ed's face turning red and knew what was coming.

"NO," he stated with authority. "You must bless the baby's room."

The priest turned to leave and Ed grabbed his shoulder and restated, "You will bless our baby's room!"

I walked with Ed and the priest as he blessed Christine's room. I didn't understand a word, for it was in Latin, and he was talking in hyper speed. He then turned and bolted toward the door, except he grabbed the wrong doorknob and walked into the closet. As I watched, I suppressed my laugh, but couldn't hide my smile. As there was a shuffle of bodies around the door, all I could see was George waving an envelope and Ed with a very unhappy expression. When the priest corrected himself, he opened the hallway door and left without a word. I saw Ed grab the envelope from George and follow the priest out the door. I really did not know about the envelope having a traditional offering; [Catholic thing] all I saw was poor, blind George trying to get his bearings, Ed grabbing the envelope, George putting out his hands trying to figure out where the envelope went, and Ed chasing the priest. It was dead silent in the room.

Ed finally returned and I could tell he was pissed. He said to me, "That priest WILL be back and he WILL bless this damned house."

During this time, some laughter broke out regarding the priest walking completely into the closet, while others questioned what exactly had happened? The festive feeling that we all had was gone as things became serious. Most were listening as Ed explained to George what happened from beginning to end. What they were hearing was that the house blessing was incomplete and the priest was an idiot, in Ed's opinion, and had screwed up everything.

The mood became solemn and I was disappointed. Our appetites had shrunk. We had spent more than we could afford for the food, and I had to send most of it away with our guests. The day we had planned and looked forward to was a complete disaster. Afterward, Ed assured me that he would call the Church and get the priest to return for a complete and proper blessing. He really didn't understand what happened. He thought the brass dispenser shattering highly unusual, but felt nothing more was behind that occurrence. He thought the priest's behavior was akin to stage fright and embarrassment. We ended that day very depressed. One thing that I became aware of was that Ed was starting to believe. He sort of gave it away with the obvious hopes that a house blessing would put things to rest. When told of how Myra had greeted the priest with a stream of foul language, I sort of predicted the priest might never return.

It seemed the attempted blessing did stir things up, as whatever was there became more active. I had no idea how many phone calls Ed made to the Church the following week, but I did witness how angry he was at the priest, the church, and all things Catholic.

"How could they refuse to bless our house?" This was something I would hear over and over again. "I will go see that priest in person."

It wasn't funny at the time, but knowing Ed, I knew visiting the priest would turn into a complete disaster...and it did. As a young man, Ed had a very short fuse and when his temper surfaced, it was explosive. I have no idea what was actually said, but the end result was our being expelled from the parish and banned from the Church grounds. All I ever got out of Ed was that Father Barnes suggested we get our heads examined and he told the priest off. If there was anything positive that came from this whole mess, it was that the blessing of our daughter's room seemed to have worked. It actually was a "safe" room. Never was she disturbed in her sleep, nor was anything ever found out of place. Christine would always be at my side, with the exception of sleeping in her room, once she established proper sleeping habits.

This whole sequence of events shattered Ed's faith in the Catholic institution. It took him from being devout, to turning his back to the organization. He was completely baffled as to how they could preach of demons and angels and miracles, yet turn their backs to anything outside of their teachings. Ed knew his bible and could quote where Jesus exorcised demons and evil spirits, so how the Catholic faith could just ignore those biblical examples made him confused and angry. He did have one good point and that was there is a frequent mention of demons, but no real mention of ghosts.

The one significant thing that I believe the visiting priest and attempted house blessing created was that it stirred the pot a bit. That day was like another declaration of war. Things became more active and more frequent. It was only days after the priest had visited, that my kitchen cabinet door opened as usual. However, this time, I nearly had to duck, as a plate came flying out. Unlike Paranormal Witness, which portrayed a stream of ceramic plates flying at me, there was only one. We were too poor to own real dishes, and what we ate off of was called Melamine, a type of plastic. These we got free for every time we spent $20 at the grocery store. You could get a cup, saucer, or plate. So the plate sailed like a Frisbee across the room.

This was very alarming, and scared the crap out of me, but it sailed well over my head since I was sitting down and seemed not intended to hurt me. I had no idea why, other than to show me who was boss. Initially, I did not tell Ed, as I envisioned him throwing all our dishes away and buying paper plates and stating, "That solves that!" It was his way of solving things. Of course, he would learn he was wrong.   Even today, I wonder why I stayed in that kitchen. My deduction is always the same, because I had my escape door just feet away and right outside was my bright, enclosed porch that I envisioned as a safe haven; my access to the outer world.

Christmas was upon us, and we had little to spend on presents, but I looked forward to Christmas shopping. At least we would be outside that house. I could not have cared less if we bought a damned thing. I just loved being out and not having the feeling of apprehension. There was a strange thing that we only realized much later. Myra had been quiet and we never saw her. We never SAW her. We never saw her go out shopping, nor did we see anyone visit and deliver groceries. When did she come and go? How did she survive? Rarely did we ever see the glow of a light bulb through a window, as her apartment was always dark. This leads us to another puzzle. We never heard her little dog bark. Plus, never did we see her letting the dog out to do its business. Knowing how protective these little dogs can be, even when Ed yelled back at Myra, the dog never acknowledged him. It was as if he wasn't there. The dog never made a whimper. Not even once. At this point, we imagined that the cleanup of this apartment when Myra moved out would be massive. Regardless, we counted the days until she would be gone! Looking back some 40+ years, both Ed and I will always wonder if that little dog even existed?

We had only been living there a few months, but it was already taking its toll. I was always paranoid and in a defensive frame of mind because of the baby. It was soon after the house blessing that I witnessed the second event happening before my eyes. We had a hand mixer that hung on a hook near the kitchen cabinet, on the wall. As I was sitting at the kitchen table, it moved slightly upward, which caught my attention. Then, it came toward me, floating in mid-air, and promptly landed at my feet. I was in shock. Obviously, I could hardly believe my eyes. Unlike in the movies, my tendency was not to scream, for I was both amazed and paralyzed.

There was no doubt what we were up against, and this was an indicator of its power. It was a new plastic hand mixer and was not that heavy, but it lifted and traveled about 4 feet. It was not like it was thrown at me, but more like someone was trying to hand it to me. I debated whether to mention it to my skeptical husband, and decided I would. Ed began coming home for lunch, and now I had something real to talk about.

I reluctantly told Ed about the mixer, to which I received his standard answer of, "Bullshit."

This resulted in an argument, regarding his denial. I was confused, because he seemed to acknowledge that things were happening that he could not explain, but rejected the whole ghost idea. In reality, he did start to believe, but his denial was so he did not feed my fears. Later, I understood that he was having trouble coping with the fact that he was leaving me alone. He was filled with guilt, but would not speak of it. I have an understanding of what and why he felt that way, but what other choice did he have? We had bills to pay and had to eat. I never understood how much he had experienced in that basement and all the information he was carrying that he would never share with me. Though getting closer, we were still traveling in separate worlds.

At this point, although Ed was always addressing Ben, I felt that I was dealing with a female. Everything indicated that, in my estimation. The mixer, the broom, the faucet, and cabinet, all seemed as things a woman might do. What Ed was dealing with, I imagined being different, because it originated in the dark, ominous basement. Whatever was down there I wanted no part of. There was no doubt in my mind that we were dealing with multiple ghosts. I knew a man had died in this apartment, but I was not sensing him…at least, not yet.

The arrival of Holly seemed to create a whole new phenomena…footsteps. I could watch Holly's ear tilt in the direction of the back porch and we would hear heavy, strong footsteps, sounding like someone coming up the back stairs. This would result in Holly giving us her warning bark, followed by Ed putting her on a leash and investigating. At first, he thought it to be Myra, but after a number of investigations, there was no explanation. It was as if they were teasing the poor dog.   As I recall, these footsteps were always happening in the evening, or late at night, but never after midnight. Our cat, Kitty, also had her events. Kitty was the only one that would sit in the living room, resting in her green velvet chair. She was not an active cat; though loveable, she preferred being on her own. So there she would sit, curled up, unless she was hungry at which time she would bother me in the kitchen.

It was one night during dinner that Ed and I clearly heard her do a loud growl. As we went to see why she was bothered, we saw her tail expand, the hair on her back bristle, and she darted out the living room, looking back and hissing. Whatever she saw went unchallenged, so we both wondered what she could see that we couldn't. She went into our bedroom, looking back at the living room, still hissing all the way. We didn't say much to each other, but knew that whatever Kitty experienced, she clearly decided that she would give up that space. Our bedroom became her new safe haven. At night, both the dog and the cat stayed with us in that room.

Our routine remained the same. I would hold up in the kitchen and Ed would try to come home as much as he could for lunch. After work, we would have a tense dinner, usually dominated by the activities within the house. Then, Ed would head for the basement or garage to work. There was a change that we never realized. When we moved in, he worked on the house until about 10 PM, then we would maybe watch the news and go to bed. As months passed, Ed worked later, sometimes as late as midnight before we went to bed. We were both becoming sleep deprived...or could it be that we really never wanted to go to sleep and be vulnerable in this house? We never shared, but I knew both of us were suffering nightmares. It was evident when he would sit up in bed in a cold sweat. I know Ed never mentioned this in the first book, but nightmares become a standard part of living in these conditions. Whether "they" were entering our dreams or our subconscious was suffering our worst fears, we didn't really know.

It was early in the new year that I heard Ed on the phone. He was telling George that he was not on the phone all night and that it was off the hook. He explained that the phone sometimes does that. It was obvious that George did not believe it, and he and Ed began arguing. Like everyone else, George's response was that we were crazy. "There are no such things as ghosts!" After Ed hung up, I could see the frustration on his face. The strange part was that as his friends heard about our house possibly being haunted, they all laughed, but they never visited. This was not unusual;

person after person either laughed, were skeptical, or downright rude with blatant ridicule.

That phone was always a problem. I laughed to myself at times when I would hear Ed arguing with George, explaining the phone coming off the hook. George just punished Ed with his comments and Ed would slam the phone down and mumble, 'asshole.' It would not be long before we would invite George and his wife over for dinner, and George would get a first hand display!

It was a night in January when our doorbell rang. I followed Ed downstairs and there stood a strange woman with a serious looking man behind her.

"Can I help you?" Ed asked.

"I was wondering if I may come in?" she replied.

"Why?"

"I believe my baby cradle is up in the attic. If you would allow me to come in, I could go to the attic and check if it is still there."

"I don't think so," Ed responded coldly.

"But if you would just let me look, it would only take a moment," she countered.

"I'm sorry, but no way. If you give me your number and I find a cradle, I will call you."

The woman wrote her phone number down on a piece of paper and handed it to Ed. He quickly closed the door and crumpled the piece of paper up. I thought it was strange.

"Why were you so abrupt?" I wondered.

"Why? Because those people have never been in this house and they could not have been family, so I have no idea what they really wanted. Besides, I didn't like the look of that silent guy standing behind her."

"How do know they aren't family?"

"If they were family and were ever here before, they would have known there is no conventional way up to the attic. You have to get a ladder, climb through the back porch roof, then open a small window with hinge. You could not get anything larger than a small box in that attic, which is exactly what I found and threw out! I don't know who they are, but she is a liar."

Ed had learned a lot about this family which he had never shared with me. On this occasion, he did.

"I heard that the father who passed away some years ago was old-school in that he did not trust banks, so he hid his money. That likely is the reason this place was torn apart when we first saw it. In the basement, there are even places where they broke into the concrete walls and patched it up. As far as anyone knows, no one ever found any money. One neighbor told me he owned some farmland in Indiana, and maybe the money is buried there," Ed laughed.

"Based on what I have seen of the condition of this building and its contents, the old man was either dead broke, or he had a shit load of money, because he certainly didn't spend any maintaining the building or buying furniture! Marsha, from what we witnessed at the closing, this family is a bunch of money grubbing, greedy people. If she was family, why didn't she ring Myra's doorbell?"

He was right, and that was something that didn't cross my mind. I felt a bit bad, because the woman had called me the previous day and asked to check the attic. I had told her it seemed okay, but she would have to ask Ed. She explained that her baby cradle might be up there and that she would appreciate getting it back as a keepsake. It all sounded so innocent. The problem was that I had no idea where the attic entrance was. I had never mentioned the call to Ed. Who they really were has always been a mystery. I knew they were not at the closing, and we never saw or heard from them again.

We were now into late winter and early 1971. When the weather allowed, I would struggle with our full size buggy down the front stairs and take the baby for a walk. I would use any opportunity I had to leave when I could. It was on one of these walks that I stopped and sat on the stairs of our local Catholic church. I frequently rested there, as I felt protected, and I appreciated the smiles from people coming and going. I was aware of the scene Ed caused with the Pastor, but what happened next shocked me.

A nun came out from the Church and as she passed me, she turned to face me and sternly said, "You have to move on, as we don't want you here."

To this day I don't know whether she was just voicing their policy on loitering, or if she recognized me as the family that was expelled from their parish. In any event, it almost made me cry that it seemed we had nowhere to turn and I lost my 'safe' place.

Looking back, it truly is hard to explain to anyone in this modern paranormal world how painful it was, always being rejected. All I wanted was a place to go where I could feel at peace, with no anxiety. I will never be sure why this nun sent me away, but we both feel that anyone who truly believes in the power of God has to have the ultimate fear of the polar opposite. I believe we represented people that could show them their worst fears, of which they wanted no reminders.

It was sometime before Myra left that I had a major explosion. Ed had come home and we were eating dinner and I had closed the door that separated the kitchen from the rest of the house. As we began eating, the old over-painted wood door opened. Ed just looked at it and continued eating...which aggravated me.

"Did you see that?"

"Yeah," he mumbled with his mouth full, continuing to eat.

"I wanted the door closed," I replied with an attitude.

"What the hell difference does it make?" Ed seemed annoyed.

"These ghosts just do whatever they like to aggravate us."

"You're the only one aggravated. Open door, closed door, who cares?" Ed really just wasn't getting it.

"They are controlling our lives and we are just becoming pawns in their game. Whatever did that did it to get us to respond. So here we are arguing about it. It gets us to argue, interrupts our dinner, and now I have to close that damned door. No sooner than I do it, it will open again."

"So what? A door opens, a broom moves, big fucking deal. Hey Ben! Cut that shit out, you fucking air bag!" Ed was mocking the whole situation. Yes, he commonly called them 'air bags' before true air bags existed!

"You're calling him by name?"

"If we have a ghost, it is that old pervert, Ben," Ed laughed.

"Ben?"

"Yeah, he left me quite a collection to clean up in the basement. Hey Ben! Quit messing with the door!"

"So just ignore things and let it all happen?"

Ed rose from the table and walked toward the door. "You want it closed? I'll close it for you."

As I watched, Ed left and came back with some heavy string. He closed the door and tied the string around the doorknob. In the woodwork was a loop that was used to hold up a gate, which we used to keep Christine from crawling out of the kitchen. He threaded the string through the loop and literally tied the door closed. There was maybe an inch of slack.

"There! The door will now stay closed."

He then returned to eating dinner, while I stared in awe. Did he really think this would stop the activity? Did he think this would not spark another event? I was upset. Before I could start another conversation, the door attempted to open. Instead, it was limited to about an inch, as the string held tight. It began vibrating. We both stared in silence. I was honestly frightened, as I imagined all kinds of things. Would the string break and the door fly open? Would the door just fly off the hinges? I knew this was not a good situation.

"Eddie, we have to do something."

Ed instantly erupted in anger. "Screw them. Screw Ben. What's the matter Ben, can't break a piece of string? Oh scary. You old pervert! See? He can't even break a piece of string. I'm shaking in my shoes. Go bother someone else, you damned pervert."

I was upset. "Stop it! Stop it! You are going to create more problems!"

"What problems? Screw whatever this is. I will kick their asses out!"

"Do you see what is happening to you? Look at you. You are talking to ghosts. You even named him. You stomp around angrily, you sit watching the bathtub plug, and bitch about the phone. You're not controlling them.....they're controlling you!"

As I spoke, the door stopped vibrating, but the kitchen lights started flickering. Ed sat down and I could tell what I had said had registered with him, but a young Ed would not admit defeat. I knew he had something going through that head of his. He finished dinner and went to work, which was painting the basement. I was frightened, because as sure as I felt that whatever was in our kitchen was female, I also felt that whatever was moving that door was male. I also knew that tying the door shut was not the right thing to do.

The next day was the same old routine. The broom was outside the pantry, the cabinet door was open, and there was a dish on the floor. All this may sound benign, but I always felt that as I responded and reacted, THEY were watching me and maybe even mocking me. I always was looking about for something else they might decide to do. I would get the baby and turn on my small TV. Then, I'd open the back door, making sure the screen door was locked so Myra couldn't barge in, and I would sit, watching TV, but always looking about. It was now all a habit. This was my normal day.

That evening, Ed came home carrying a box that he put in the bathroom. I was curious.

"What is that?"

"You'll see. It is my solution to that damned plug. You were right, and me sitting in the bathroom watching the plug is over. You seem to think these things are not solvable, but they are. After today, there will be no more watching the plug and no more drinking my morning coffee in the bathroom!"

I wanted to believe him, but knew all these things did not have solutions. I also believed that if he did halt any single activity, that it would initiate a new one and one that we could not predict. In a way, he was upping their game. Today, Ed freely admits that he was wrong in how he reacted, and does believe he fueled much of the activity.

We sat to have dinner, and the kitchen door slowly opened. Without a word, Ed got up and closed it, tying the string so that it would not open. It began vibrating before he even sat down. Ed just looked at it and laughed, then continued eating. He had me worried, as although he acknowledged certain things, he would not admit we had a problem. Somehow, he felt he was in control, or at least that was the image he wanted me to believe. After dinner he went to work in the bathroom.

Our bathtub was a free standing, old claw foot iron tub. Actually, it was the style people pay huge amounts for today. All the plumbing was exposed, and Ed began tearing the drain pipes out. In the box was a new drainage system. It was the kind with a lever that moves up and down, opening and closing the plug. It was no more than an hour and he was finished.

"Come look at this. I set the lever to make it as hard to open and close as I could. Let's see them mess with it now!"

Honestly, I did not know what to think, but we would surely find out in the morning. On this night, Ed was outside on the enclosed back porch, where he was painting. I remember it was a nice evening, as I watched TV. Ed was right outside within sight, which made me feel secure. The next morning, I woke him up and he went to the bathroom and started his bath water. He proceeded to join me in the kitchen for coffee just like we did before the whole bathtub debacle. He never went to check and appeared totally confident that the tub would remain filled with hot water. He was correct. When he went to his bath, the tub was filled. He boasted, "I guess this is one for Ed!"

Whatever the fixation with the old rubber plug, Ed was correct that installing a new modern trip lever was the solution. He seemed blind to the overall threat and consequences. He would get agitated, annoyed, and even angry, but he never felt fearful or showed it. I didn't understand it, because I knew these little things would escalate and hoped it would not become dangerous.

Ed was always amused by the vibrating kitchen door and in fact, when it did not vibrate, he would call out to Ben to try to open it. It was typical for Ed to be eating dinner and in a raised voice he would call, "Ben? Ben come out and open the door. Come on Ben, you can do it." In most cases, the door would begin vibrating and trying to open. Ed would laugh and mock 'Ben' as being weak, lame, and a poor excuse for a ghost. I would always get upset and ask him to stop.

It was one evening when he was on the phone with George. Of course, they were arguing about whether spirits even exist. He invited George and his wife for dinner, claiming he would prove it. So a few days later George and his wife showed up. After dinner, we sat and talked, catching up on each other's lives. They also had a new daughter, born the same month as ours. Eventually, the conversation shifted to Ed's claim of ghosts. It was George that brought it up.

"Okay, show me something that proves you have ghosts." He turned to his wife. "Ed claims his ghost takes the phone off the hook."

I always thought it unusual that Ed and George interacted as if George was not blind.

"Here, I'll show you something." Ed arose and closed the kitchen door, tying it shut as he always did.

"What's he doing?" George asked.

"He just closed the kitchen door to the front of the house and tied it shut," his wife explained.

Ed returned to the table and stated, "Watch that door and listen."

Ed began calling out. "Ben? You there? Come on Ben, open the door."

George began rolling in laughter. "You gave it a name? You are completely crazy!" George nudged his wife. "He gave it a name!" George was totally amused, while Ed continued calling out. The more Ed called out, the more George mocked him.

Then it began. The knob turned and the door attempted to open. It suddenly became very quiet. George's wife whispered to George. "The door is moving." As all of us focused our attention on the door, it began vibrating. It started slowly, as usual, and became faster and faster, as if whatever was doing it was in a frenzy. George's wife became excited. "George, it's vibrating." His wife's eyes were as big as can be. After a time, it suddenly stopped. For a moment all was silent before George began ridiculing Ed.

"You are nuts. So a door vibrates a little and you say it is a ghost? Let me see that door."

His wife led him to the door and George examined it with his hands. She led him back to the table. "All I can say is what a crock of shit! I still say there is no such thing. It is all bullshit."

George and his wife had their backs to our kitchen cabinet. Between the top of the cabinet and the ceiling, Ed had installed some wooden spindles. Behind the spindles were some fake flowers and some fake vines. Only Ed saw what was coming, as he was facing the cabinet. A single spindle floated from behind George and his wife, over their heads. As Ed flinched, it came from about an 8 foot height and slammed straight down to the center of the table.

"What the hell was that?"

I think all of us spoke at the same time.

"A piece of wood?" George's wife stated.

"That spindle just flew over us and fell on the table," I gasped.

"Guess whatever it was does not like being laughed at," Ed stated dryly.

"Let me feel that thing," George asked.

What he felt was a heavy wood spindle, about 1 ½ inches thick and about 2 feet long. George never said a word after feeling it. I could only imagine the fear a blind man might feel knowing things can just be thrown at him without warning. Ed sat, serious and in thought. It actually may have been the first time he realized what could possibly happen, and the anxiety I was suffering. George and his wife left immediately afterward and never returned for a visit again. Ed took the spindle and dropped it on the table, watching it roll or bounce every single time. He kept repeating the action.

"It was like someone slammed it down on the table..." Ed stated in confusion. "When I drop it, it bounces and rolls. You cannot drop this thing and have it sit on the table without it moving in some way. It never moved. It was like someone slammed it down on the table and held it there...not like it was dropped. That sucker was nailed to the ceiling. Where the hell is the nail?" Ed paced it off and estimated it flew horizontally about 4 feet before coming straight down. For once, he had no way to apply logic. There was no way to rationalize the cause. Ed was stumped.

To this day, the whole occurrence remains a mystery. What caused it will always be a mystery, but I wondered why it did not hit anyone? I absolutely knew there were more spirits than just one, so could one be kind? Later I would learn that one was kind and benign. This was likely done by the old woman, who resented being mocked, but meant no harm. It would only be a short matter of time before I would correlate the fact that every time I scolded Christine or tapped her little bottom, there would be an activity. I assumed the old woman didn't like it and it was her only way of letting me know.

I was just looking forward to Myra moving out and having some normal people in the building. I knew that even Ed had to wonder that with

Myra always cradling her little dog, was it a familiar? Was Myra a witch? Was all this the work of Myra? We would soon know.

CHAPTER THREE

"Never torment or tease a spirit, for it will most certainly return the gesture."

Dave, 2012

It was a mild February in Chicago, and we looked forward to Myra leaving. When I think back, we experienced all the routine activity, but we had many calm days. Ed had made it a habit of coming home for lunch and a lot of his work was done on the enclosed back porch, so in the evenings, he was always right outside the back door, within calling distance. He did make an effort in contacting a few other parishes in an attempt to get a Catholic priest to bless the house, but it became my impression that each parish was like a separate franchise, and unless a family was registered within a parish, the priests only serviced those registered families. So, he failed.

Even though I was raised Episcopal and Baptist, I never suggested Ed approach a priest or minister of another denomination. I pretty much envisioned the same result he had with the Catholics. Likely, we would be called disturbed and turned away. There is something about being shunned by the ones that provide your faith that makes you feel like your situation is fatal.

No doubt, we had changed. We simply accepted a certain amount of activity. It wasn't so much like we ignored it, but more as if it was no longer alarming. I would simply put the broom back where it belonged. Open or closed, I now I paid little attention to the cabinet door. The only real thing that startled me was that every now and then a Melamine dish would come sailing out. If I found the kitchen faucet on, I turned it off. Ed continued playing with tying the kitchen door, which always upset me, but his new drain plug eliminated the problem in the bath tub.

One of the things that continued and became routine, were the footsteps on the back porch. They made no sense, as the outer door into the porch was always locked, so no one could get in. The logical answer was Myra; but the footsteps were too heavy, and Myra's door was always locked, with no lights on in her apartment. The heavy footsteps were always in the evening or at night, typically right after we had gone to bed. The sound would always set Holly off, and she would begin barking warnings. This forced Ed to take her to the porch and satisfy her that no one was there, for if he didn't, she would continue growling.

All this may seem strange, but this life became our new 'normal.' If I observed something unusual, like an object that was moved, I merely put it back in place. I knew Ed was experiencing things in the basement, but he would never share. One thing I knew about Ed, was that he 'needed' music, but despite the many nights he worked down there emptying junk, cleaning and painting, he never took a radio with him. Given the many hours he spent in that dark basement, it was obvious he wanted to hear and always be aware of his surroundings, so he worked in dead silence. He never stated a thing...but I knew.

We were very conditioned. We were now familiar with all the signals that the body sends you. I knew when an entity entered the room, and I knew when I was being watched. More and more, Ed would think of a reason that we had to go shopping. We were living hand to mouth, so if we received a dinner invitation, we were there without hesitation. We were anxious for Myra to leave, as we could soon lease her apartment and begin collecting rent, which would make life much easier.

At this point, we had no idea that there was any activity within the first floor apartment. We knew an old man died in ours, and figured that was the source of our problems. Never did the thought of our future renters being bothered enter our minds. One argument we had, was that I wanted to return to work. Besides the obvious benefit of having more money, I could be out of the house. Ed would not bend on this subject, because he did not trust anyone to care for our baby, aside from family. Daycare was out of the question in his mind, until Christine could talk. It was not a chauvinistic thing; it was that he was an abused child and did not trust our daughter to anyone. I was not happy, but I understood, because this was something we both agreed on before she was ever born. I agreed at that time, because I never imagined being in the situation we were in.

We had no notice, but it was the last day in February that Myra was finally moved out. We saw the moving truck parked in front of the building and movers emptying the apartment. We watched and celebrated silently. They led Myra out, carrying her little dog. It was obvious that she was not happy as they put Myra in the back of a car and she twisted her head to stare at the building. We could still see her staring out as the car pulled away. Despite our negative clashes, I felt sad for Myra, as she was leaving the only home she had ever known. Once they were all out of sight, we hurried downstairs to view what we anticipated as a possible cleaning disaster.

The apartment door was unlocked, and to our surprise, the place was completely empty. With the exception of dust and minor clutter, and the fact that the floors hadn't been washed in years…it was fairly clean. It appeared they even swept up a bit. Ed immediately looked for traces of possible dog messes, and found none. In fact, there was no trace a dog had ever been there. Unlike how we found our place, this apartment was clean.

Ed was very anxious to rent, and wanted immediately to put an ad in the Chicago paper. I was against it, because we had agreed to clean it up and even paint it before renting. It didn't take long before he got his bucket, a scrub brush, and a gallon of disinfectant, and was soon preparing to scrub the whole floor on his knees. That is where he would spend his next day off, scrubbing every inch. It was during this time that he experienced something he failed to hide. All I knew was that he came running upstairs asking me, "What happened?"

I had no clue what he was talking about. He related that he was in the basement filling the bucket in the laundry sink, and had heard a heavy crash above his head, like a piece of furniture had fallen or been dropped. He knew the kitchen above him was empty, and assumed it came from our apartment.

He couldn't hide his confusion as he kept repeating, "It was loud! It shook the house…it was right over my head…"

He could not believe that I had not heard a thing, and I could see the confusion in his face. He finished working on the apartment and aside from needing a coat of paint, all was clean. The floors were clean, the windows were sparkling, and I assumed the next weekend would be spent painting.

There was something I sensed and it was that Ed had an upsetting experience. Whether it was that loud crash, or whether he had seen something, I knew it was significant because he spent the evening withdrawn and in thought. He did put the ad in the paper, which he didn't relay to me.

The following Monday our ad started. It had only been hours when our phone rang. It was a woman named Ellen. She was inquiring whether she and her husband could come and see the apartment. I assumed Ed must have submitted the ad, but I didn't want anyone to see the apartment until it was painted, yet I reluctantly agreed. When Ed arrived home that evening I gave him the news. I voiced my displeasure about showing the place before it had been painted, but he had a solution.

"If they want the place, we will offer to pay for the paint and let them choose their own colors. They will be happier, and we won't have the extra work. I will even give them a break on the rent."

Personally, I felt like it was something we should do, but Ed had a list of repairs and chores as long as his arm, so if this solution would work, it was better for him. I had never been a landlady before, and I certainly was not used to presenting demands or negotiating.

The next day, Ellen rang the bell. She looked much younger than her age and her baby was so tiny. I was immediately happy, as we had instant chemistry. I gave Ellen the tour. Even though it needed a fresh coat of paint, she seemed happy with the whole arrangement. She said it was larger than where they had been living and was happy to have the laundry area in the basement. I knew that Ed said to maintain a distance, but Ellen and I became friends instantly. It was a pleasure to have someone there I could talk with.

Ellen had brought along a baby walker, which I thought was cute, but it served to be more like a baby holder, since her tiny baby's feet did not touch the floor, so the walker-part didn't apply. Ed had brought a table and two chairs into the empty apartment and had put them in the kitchen, where we sat. It was almost like I was imagining this, because the baby's feet were dangling, but the walker was slowly moving on its own. Since Ellen had her back to the baby, she could not see anything was happening. Suddenly, I realized the walker was moving toward the open door, which led to the basement stairs. There was no doubt the baby was going to tumble down the stairs. I may have startled Ellen as I moved so quickly and pulled the walker in mid-air back toward me. The front wheels were already over the edge when I grabbed it. My heart was pounding and hands were shaking, yet I kept as calm of an expression as I could.

It is a moment such as this when you question whether a sinister force is in play, or whether the floor was just not level. In any event, Ellen didn't take notice and I moved the walker close to me, watching in hopes that it would not move again. It may sound strange, but I had no clue that this first floor apartment was also occupied. Ellen was delighted and could not wait to show her husband. I really felt good, because now I would have someone to talk with. She left with a smile.

Please understand that at this time we had no idea that each apartment had its own ghosts. I was paranoid and my belief was that they were following me. Ed, at that time, believed it was one ghost moving about the building and it was fixated on us. We both had no idea of the number of spirits we were dealing with, and the fact that they each dominated their own space within the building.

That evening, Dave and Ellen rang the bell. We invited them in and went to our kitchen, where I offered them coffee. Ed had all these things he was going to do, such as check their references etc., but it all went out the window when they related their story. They had a baby and were being kicked out of their apartment. Sound familiar? Their baby was the same age as ours and as they continued, we were stunned. First, their obstetrician was the same one as ours. Then, we found that their daughter was born at the exact same hospital as ours. This almost seemed more than coincidence, because in this city of millions of people and a vast number of hospitals, they also chose Skokie Valley Hospital, a small, relatively unknown hospital outside Chicago. Finally, Ellen and I were there only a week apart.

As Ellen and I conversed, Ed and Dave also talked a mile a minute as both were working in the field of technology. Both were on the ground floor of emerging fields; Ed in computers, and Dave in surveillance. Dave's current job was setting up surveillance cameras in the brand new Schaumburg

Mall. Dave was also an electronic wizard and could fix almost anything. Ed tried to maintain a distance, as they were to be our renters, but I could tell he liked them both.

We walked downstairs and showed them the apartment. I explained that we had intended to paint, but if they wanted, they could paint it and we would pay for the paint and they could choose their own colors. They agreed immediately. I expected Ed to have them fill out the application that he had prepared, but instead, he offered his hand and they shook on it. Dave wrote out the checks for security and first month's rent, signed the lease, and we now had our new tenants.

I felt so great, as Ellen was near my age. She was sweet and talkative, plus we shared the fact of being new mothers. I knew Ellen and I would be sharing coffee on a regular basis. Ed and I never consciously withheld the paranormal activity, but honestly, it was such a relief to have normal people in the building; it was like we hoped that all would be normal, and that everything was gone with Myra. Ed, especially, felt that Myra was some kind of witch. He didn't know much about these things, but since he found a well worn Ouija board [that he never told me about] he suspected the family dabbled in the occult.

We were ecstatic, as our new tenants were perfect, and we now had some extra income to make our lives easier. The few dollars may not seem like much today, but in 1971, canned goods were still 10 cents for the most part, and bread was 20 cents a loaf...so a few dollars really went a long way. The one thing I vividly remember was that my whole grocery budget was now increased to 25 dollars a week. Just as a reference, gas was at about 30 cents a gallon and cigarettes had just increased to $2.50 a carton. Yes, things were much different in 1971.

Both Dave and Ellen were anxious to move, so they moved in mid-March. Dave's employer was relocating their company close by, so Dave was really happy with his new location. I couldn't contain myself, in that I invited Ellen for coffee as soon as I could. It was our first morning after they moved in that Ellen came up for a chat. The day seemed to pass by in a flash as we shared our backgrounds, with everything from growing up, to how we met our husbands. It was right off that I had to tell her about our ghost. I told her it was not something that was your conventional type of scary, but the activity I experienced was annoying. She seemed very interested as I explained how a man had died in our apartment and that his spirit may still be here.

Yes, it was easy to talk of ghosts with Ellen. What was the image of a ghost in 1971? I can say with authority that they were typically portrayed as a white sheet with two holes for eyes. That was the scariest image one could imagine in 1971. The alternative was friendly ghosts, like Casper, Topper, The Canterville Ghost, or that handsome ghost from Mrs. Muir. The actions were startling, but the image, not so much. Today, because of Hollywood, the images that can be imagined can be very, very frightening.

It was then that Ellen told me that Dave was very superstitious. He was native Canadian, and his mother was a full blooded Mohawk. So I was warned by Ellen not to speak of such things. We agreed that talking about ghosts to Dave would be taboo. We decided there was no reason not to have dinner together, so when the men came home, they would join us. I also figured it was good for Ed to get break from his constant working on the house.

Over dinner, we learned a lot about our new tenants. Dave had Ed mesmerized as he related his native beliefs and ghost stories he was told as a child. He stated that these were not stories to scare little children, but were remembered and practiced into adulthood. One thing for sure, we did not relate anything he spoke of to our situation at that time. Instead of understanding that Dave had a solid grasp of the paranormal within his culture, we assumed it was all folklore, and did not apply to us.

I noticed that Dave kept looking at Ed's right hand and studying him. Only later would I learn that he focused on a ring that Ed wore on his pinky finger. It was a black star sapphire, and the black stone was regarded as bad luck. Dave would later warn Ed of this. I have no idea whether Ed believed him at that time, but today the ring sits in our safe-deposit box.

With Native Canadians, or Americans, the spirit world is taken seriously and is never a laughing matter. They need no proof, nor do they want any! This was a huge factor in what was to come, because Ellen would never tell Dave of anything she experienced. She would keep it to herself. In retrospect, it was very strange that Ed would keep things from me, I would keep things from him, and now Ellen would keep things from Dave. Our ghosts had the perfect scenario to divide and conquer.

On the back porch under the stairs on the first floor was a small storage room. Dave asked if he could use it as his workshop. Of course, we had no problem with that, so he moved a work table in and set up his tools for his projects.

Once they moved in, we hoped all would be put to rest with Myra being gone. In all honesty, we felt that whatever we were plagued with was primarily unique to our apartment, if only because of the death we knew that took place there. Soon after Ellen and Dave were moved in, despite what Ed warned me about in getting too close to our tenants, Ellen and I began having coffee on a regular basis. Most times, it was Ellen that came upstairs to knock on my door. Soon, I left the door unlocked so she could come and go at will. It could have been the ideal situation with all our compatibilities, and the fact that our daughters immediately acted like sisters.

It was within the first week when we were sharing coffee that Ellen became serious. She asked if Ed and I had been getting along. I was a bit taken back at first, wondering why she might even ask that. Ellen explained that they could hear arguing, which sounded like it was coming from our apartment. As she spoke, I already knew what she was hearing, because we also had been hearing it on a regular basis. We thought it was coming from their apartment or the back porch, but Ed rationalized it was likely coming from the building next door. It did not take long before they were hearing it when we were not home. We never thought they were bothered, because when Ellen was in my kitchen, all was calm and there was hardly a mention of paranormal activity.

Reality was that it was Dave that became a target immediately. Did they sense his beliefs? It began in his little workshop under the stairs. He had set it up with all his tools and supplies to fix electronic devices, and many surveillance cameras and recorders. It was only days after it was set up that he would find things out of place. At first, nothing was missing, so he imagined it was Ed being curious and moving things around. He never locked the workshop, as the outer door to the enclosed porch was always locked, so his assumption was that if anything was disturbed, it was someone from the inside. Ellen was also suffering some activity, as she would spend more and more time visiting, but was keeping it to herself. Why? After talking with Dave 42 years later, he told of Ellen being tormented, but by what? Whatever the experience, to this day, it remains her secret.

It was soon after they had moved in when Ed came home for lunch and asked, "Who is the old lady sitting out front on our stairs?"

I had no idea, so he led me to the front windows and as we both looked out, he began scratching his head, as she was gone. In Chicago, it was never unusual for an older person to go shopping and take a rest by sitting on the stairs of a building. However, as it continued, Ed would ask "Who is that old woman?" He would then take me to the front windows and we would both look down and see nothing. Ed never was alarmed; he was just curious. It was only a few weeks later that one morning he was late and rushing out the front door. I ran to kiss him goodbye and we were standing on the landing. We both looked at the base of the stairs and there stood an old woman. She appeared sad or concerned, and was staring directly at us.

Ed whispered, "Can you see her?"

I whispered back, "Yes."

"That's her," he replied. "That's the old woman."

She turned and moved around the corner toward the first floor apartment. Ed said quietly, "That's it! She belongs to Dave or Ellen. That is the old woman that I have been seeing on the stairs."

Ed never said anymore, but later I would learn that he was bothered, because when she disappeared, he never heard the sound of a door opening or closing. The outer door was noisy and it would have been obvious had she exited outside, and there was no sound of the apartment door opening or closing. She just turned into the alcove and literally disappeared. That day, when having coffee with Ellen, I learned that there was no old lady was staying with them. I knew that we had absolutely seen an apparition.

She appeared as solid as can be. If we had gotten a picture, it would not be frightening, as it was just an old woman. In a way, I could not wait to tell Ed and see how he could possibly explain it. When I did tell him, it was one of a few times where he became very serious. Seeing a solid apparition will change your life. This old woman was rather ordinary, as she had gray hair pulled back as if in a bun, and a black woolen coat buttoned all the way to the top. We could not see her shoes, as they may have dated her, had they been laced, but the steps blocked out that view. If we had to put her within a time frame, she resembled any old woman from 1890 to the (then) current times. We still cannot decide whether her expression was sadness, or content?

You see, nothing is frightening about a solid apparition except, for the fact that you know it is not real. The truth is that if you have taken pictures of large crowds, you may have captured an apparition or two, but you will never know it. Hollywood has you believing they are frightening, and accompanied by all kinds of sharp sounds and special effects, but they were once people like you and me and will appear so. Maybe the only thing to fear is that they might appear when you least expect it!

I learned from Ellen that Dave wanted to talk to Ed. Dave thought Ed was intentionally turning off the electricity. Dave treasured his records and felt it might be Ed's way of letting him know he was playing them too loud.

The problem was that this could ruin his records, but it did not sound like anything Ed would do. What we did not know was that Dave was building a profile of Ed. Dave always saw Ed as being a bit agitated, and also thought Ed was 'borrowing' his tools, as after only a few weeks, his tools went from being moved around, to some completely missing. Dave was far too polite to accuse Ed of anything, but did approach him soon after about the electricity being turned off.

Dave had a strong belief in the supernatural and it seemed that these spirits understood this and exploited it, because 42 years later, we found that Dave was the main target for a period of time. In his workshop under the stairs, he would hear what he thought was us, arguing. A few times it seemed so violent that he would come upstairs and as he did, it would stop. He never mentioned this to Ellen, and kept it to himself. It was common to hear footsteps coming down the stairs directly overhead. He would hear the footsteps and he would open the door of the workroom and see nothing. Dave would often hear things and initially think it was us.

It seemed that frequently, when he would work late, he would sleep in. Ellen might go for a walk or go shopping and Dave would be awakened by thunderous sounds coming from his living room area. The first few times it happened, he arose to find the chandelier in the dining room swinging back and forth, as if something upstairs had created a strong vibration.

Much like Ed, Dave either blamed us for these occurrences or rationalized them in some way. What he did not know was that Ellen had her secrets also, most of which were never shared with anyone, including me. Today, I know that Ellen put on the bravest face of all. Whatever she was experiencing was destroying her emotionally, a little bit at a time, and she would soon break. She did share certain events, as she thought her daughter might be seeing something, but never did she tell Dave.

Dave would only take so much before he caught Ed coming home and was obviously upset about the electricity going on and off. Ed had no idea what Dave was talking about, because each apartment had a separate fuse box, and Ed had no reason to touch theirs. This caused Dave to worry about the wiring, since the building was so old. Dave also had another electrical problem. While watching his new color TV, at random times, huge black horizontal lines would interrupt his viewing. Once again, he blamed Ed, because Ed had an organ that Dave had named "The Beast." He named it that because it was an old church organ with huge tubes, opposed to transistors. Dave assumed Ed's use of this organ created the viewing interruption. Again, having separate wiring in each apartment would prevent anything like this. To Dave's knowledge, this only happened when he was watching the TV alone, and never when he was watching with Ellen.

Dave would come home and enter the kitchen and feel the heat radiating from the stove. He would touch the oven door and it would be warm, as if it had been used. At first, he imagined that Ellen had made something for dinner, but would soon find out that Ellen had not used the stove at all. It took him weeks to correlate that this only happened when Ellen was not home or in the apartment. It worried him a bit, because in the days before the electronic ignitions there was always gas running on the pilot light.

It seemed that Dave was attracting more attention and activity than any of us. By the time he had been living here a month, he was bombarded with strange events. It was funny that he attributed many to Ed. Dave would hear Ed working in the basement and come down the stairs from the first floor. Many times, he decided not to talk with Ed, because he would see him hunched over because of the low ceiling and it seemed he was talking to himself. Initially, he really wondered if Ed was just a bit crazy. Plus, Ed wore that ring with the black stone, which Dave interpreted as a dark force. In a way, I believe Ed was affected, for he was always agitated and blaming everything on 'Ben.' He would not hesitate to just randomly call Ben names or insult the family.

What we were totally unaware of was that Dave and Ellen were having significant problems. Ellen never gave me a clue that this was happening, but just as Ed was blaming me for the phone being off the hook, Dave would come home to have something of his in disarray. On more than one occasion, he returned home to have the tapes on his reel-to-reel tape recorder unwound and all over the floor. He would get upset at Ellen for allowing the baby to play with his tapes, but much like Ed and the phone, Ellen had no clue that the tapes were unwound. It also seemed that they always had a problem with the door that led to the basement. Though it had a dead bolt, which Dave would always secure, he frequently would find it unlocked or even open. It became an arguing point, as he blamed Ellen and wondered why she was always going in the basement? The spirits were working very hard at separating Dave and Ellen and ruining their relationship.

It would be over 40 years later on the set of Paranormal Witness, that Ed and I would learn that these ghosts were working on Dave and Ellen the same way they were working on us. Although Dave would reveal certain happenings to Ellen, she would keep all her torments locked inside.

It was a few months after they moved in that they began getting calls at all hours. In these years, there was no caller ID, so it was frustrating, being woken up by a loud telephone and hearing only a dial tone. This began happening frequently, so Dave eventually called the telephone company and asked for a complete list of incoming calls. To his surprise, none of the calls that were hang-ups were on the list. It didn't make any sense, as they received calls, yet the phone company's records did not reflect any. Dave began to wonder if their crank calls had any correlation with our phone being off the hook. Was this their new phone game?

This was a strange event, in that we all knew Dave was very superstitious and we all hid many happenings from him. What all of us were unaware of was Dave seemed to realize what we were dealing with and had an awareness that was at a higher level than any of us. Although he was fooled at first in thinking that much of the activity was due to Ed, he quickly realized that the supernatural was at play. It was almost like the spirits knew that they could easily affect Dave, so his experiences began to escalate. Much like Ed and I did not share our events, neither did Dave and Ellen, and for the same reasons. Dave did not want to scare Ellen, and Ellen did not want to frighten Dave.

Most people may not believe this, but during our coffee talks, we rarely spoke of paranormal events. It was like we used our time talking as an escape from our dilemma. Our children would play and we would share all the subjects that young women might talk about. I most always found Ellen smiling and upbeat and had no clue of the degree of torment that she was suffering and neither did Dave. With both Ed and Dave working long hours, we spent more time together than either of the men knew.

We knew nothing of Dave's misplaced and missing tools. We knew nothing of the frequency that his electricity was going on and off. We knew nothing of the moving chandelier or of the oven door, or the black streaks across the TV screen. All this and more we learned at dinner when filming Paranormal Witness, 42 years later.

As far as I was concerned, life was a bit easier as far as coping, and I looked forward to Ellen's visits. With the rent coming in, our life became slightly easier and we took to leaving the apartment on Sundays, which was Ed's only day off. We would visit friends, relatives, window shop, or go to the zoo, just anything that kept us out of the apartment. What we were never fully aware of, was that when we left, Ellen and Dave began hearing crashes and sounds like furniture being thrown around overhead. They did inform us of it once, but they were hearing it on a regular basis. Dave admits that, initially, he thought that somehow Ed was the source of many of these things, so he had the idea that he would get a dog. Dave wanted a large dog with an even larger bark.

So Dave went shopping and settled on a pedigreed Afghan. This is a huge breed that is a great family dog, and very protective. Dave found it humorous that the dog took to sitting on the sofa with its front paws on the floor…it was that big! They named her Stephanie, and she took to her name immediately. Dave now had confidence that anyone approaching or any unexplained noises would be heard by Stephanie, and they would get a warning bark, so he felt they had a cloak of protection.

What Dave had not counted on was the fact that animals can see and sense these things. He took notice when Stephanie brought her tail down and avoided the first bedroom, which was the dark room under the stairs. He watched Stephanie investigate every corner of the house, except that room. He also noticed that although they kept the door to the basement closed, Stephanie avoided it and treated it as if it wasn't even there.

The first night, Stephanie decided to sleep at the foot of their bed in the second bedroom. Dave watched as Stephanie would lift her head and stare at the door, as if seeing something and deciding whether to give an alert. Regardless, Dave felt that Stephanie made him feel more secure. Dave never knew what happened during the second day, but Stephanie seemed insecure when he returned home. He asked Ellen if anything happened, but she denied there was any event with Stephanie. All Dave knew was that Stephanie stayed at his side.

On the third day when Dave returned from work, Stephanie had her tail down and was constantly in a defensive mode. Once again, Dave did not understand it, but Stephanie would stare at the baby's room and growl, as if something threatening was in there. It was this night that he chose to work in his shop on the back porch. Stephanie took a position on the floor next to the door. Dave was in deep concentration, working on the circuit of a camera, when all hell broke loose. First came a deep growl from Stephanie, and Dave instantly heard footsteps overhead. Stephanie continued growling while staring at the stairs.

It was Dave's assumption that Ed would come walking down the stairs, which would be a surprise to Ed, because he never told us that they had gotten a dog. Instead, next came the arguing from overhead, and Stephanie began barking and growling. When Dave got up to investigate, he saw nothing. He walked half way up the stairs and saw that no one was there, yet Stephanie was going wild.

Dave wasn't sure what to think, except Stephanie sensed something she didn't like and felt it was an obvious threat. Dave abandoned his project and decided to watch TV. Instead of the dog sitting on the couch as usual, Stephanie cowered next to the couch, jerking her head in different directions, as if paranoid. That night when going to bed, as he and Ellen settled in, Stephanie stared at the door and began growling. Dave was confused, as there was nothing in sight and things were quiet.

Frustrated, he returned to bed and Stephanie continued to growl while looking at the door from time to time. It was early the next morning that Dave let Stephanie out to the back yard to do her business. As he watched, the huge hound bounded passed the grass, down the sidewalk adjacent to the garage, and easily jumped the back gate. Dave took off after her. By the time he reached the gate, Stephanie was nowhere in sight.

Dave ran to the mouth of the alley and could see the dog already two blocks away. He ran back to the house and got his car keys and took off in the direction of Stephanie. Dave was driving as fast as he could, and when he reached where he last saw Stephanie, there was no dog in sight. He spent time driving in all directions, but Stephanie was long gone. He had lost his prized Afghan. Strangely, this was never mentioned to us, so it was 42 years later that we learned that Dave and Ellen even had a dog!

Ellen never told Dave what she was experiencing, but he understood she was being tormented by something. Much like Ed, he attributed the mood changes and signs of depression as the aftereffects of being a new mother. Unlike Ellen, Dave was taught to respect spirits, not to fear them, so even if he recognized the activity, his belief was that if he did not participate or attempt to change it, it would pass until it literally touched him!

He was in the shop working and Ellen had taken the baby and went shopping. It was completely quiet until he heard the sound of what he thought was a woman sniffling. He listened closely, and it became clear that it was a woman crying. Dave thought it was me crying out on the back porch. He stopped working and closed the workshop and turned to go up the stairs to see if he could do anything. As he approached the base of the stairs, suddenly he felt arms grabbing him and in a second, he was being embraced by something he could not see. He was frozen in place. When something like this happens, seconds can seem like minutes, yet Dave swore he stood embraced and motionless for nearly a full two minutes. He explained that it was not like being grasped; more like a warm hug. As suddenly as it occurred, it stopped and was gone.

Although shaken by the experience, Dave did not feel like it was anything "dark," as in his beliefs, the embrace was positive and did not feel it was meant to scare him…but it did. It was the first time anything like that had ever happened to him and he reasoned it truly was an embrace, as if it was a woman clinging to him. Ellen's mother arrived for a visit, but there was no way that Dave was going to tell Ellen of the event, for he felt she would surely think he was crazy. Dave knew for sure that it was a female spirit that had somehow attached itself to him. Obviously, he did not enjoy the experience, so he began avoiding working in his shop under the stairs. In his native interpretation, it did not attempt to scare him, nor was the embrace painful, but he did not want to attract whatever it was that clung to him.

This is indicative of a haunting, as Dave hid things from Ellen, for fear she might think he was crazy, and Ellen was clearly hiding her experiences from Dave. We never have gotten Ellen's complete story, since she only shared a fraction of her experiences with me over coffee. In retrospect, it is a valid assumption that if Dave felt the embrace of a spirit, then it was likely that Ellen had also been touched. It might be hard to believe, but here we were, four adults, all keeping secrets, for fear of being ridiculed. It wouldn't stay this way forever, but for now we all had our little secrets.

As far as Ed and I at this point, we knew very little. We had no idea that Dave had any experiences and they owned or lost a dog. We thought Ellen and Dave were happy, and observed no friction in their marriage. Ed was totally unaware of our tenant's problems, or if he was, he never spoke of them. He likely kept it inside, for fear of scaring me. His agitation showed from holding it all in and not being able to do anything about our circumstances. What he hid best was that he was falling into depression and despair.

CHAPTER FOUR

"Erase all the images created by Hollywood and TV in the last 45 years...all I was left to imagine was the image of a dead old man. A dead man touched me!"

Marsha Becker, 2015

Dave visited his workshop on the back porch and found things moved and out of order and wondered if the spirit was angry that he abandoned the shop, as he was no longer blaming Ed. He was slightly confused, but decided it was best to move the whole workshop into the back bedroom. There, at least, he would not hear the arguing, crying and footsteps. He had no fear, but felt he did not want to have contact with these spirits, if he could avoid it. No one responded to his ad for a lost dog and knowing how loving and expensive an Afghan is, he assumed whoever found Stephanie would likely just keep her.

His 'embrace' on the back porch was something he wanted to share, but he felt his wife would never understand. He even felt she may think him insane! All he could think about were the words of his grandparents; that good spirits are nothing to fear, and his interpretation of that embrace seemed more warm than frightening. However, in seeing the mess in his workshop under the stairs, it appeared something was angry, since he was no longer visiting there. Was this spirit attached to him? If so, was it confined to the rear of the house? What could have happened that held this spirit there?

Spending more time at home, he began to notice changes in Ellen. Her perpetual smile faded away and she became edgy for no reason that Dave could understand. Ellen had shared a few events with me, but never did it seem to scare or alarm her. She had told me about her baby looking out and even extending her arms, as if asking something unseen to pick her up. I have since come to believe that very young children can see these things. When she visited me for coffee, our conversations and subjects took us away from our predicament...or so I always thought. Now, it was June, and everyone seemed normal, except Ed. Ed knew he could not stop all the activity and was angry that he couldn't just evict these ghosts in some way. Today, he freely admits that he had no understanding of what he was dealing with, and that he was doing all the wrong things.

We never knew what was happening just below us. Ellen approached Dave and wanted to leave our building. She was dead serious. Dave was shocked, for despite his encounters and dealing with his 'crazy' landlord, he was close to work and he knew the difficulty of finding another place to rent that would accept small children. Their talks became serious and frequent, with Ellen almost projecting an urgency, which confused Dave. Dave wondered if Ellen was having trouble with us as landlords. Did she not like the neighborhood? Did Ellen and I have a falling out?

Because of his encounters, Dave wondered if Ellen had experiences that frightened her. He attempted to try to get her to communicate about this, but all he received in return was that she urgently wanted to leave.

It was during this time that our dog began to be terrorized. It was after 10 PM when Holly jumped from the floor, onto the bed. I remember her staring at the door and hearing her growl in a way I had never heard. Ed was alarmed, because although she stared at the doorway, a dog can sense other dangers, so he wondered if someone was in the hallway or on the porch. He got up and put the leash on Holly, and she reluctantly followed him out to inspect the whole premises. Usually, when he put on her leash, she would wag and be happy, for she knew they were going on a walk; but this time, he tugged at her to follow.

Only a decade later did Ed admit it was one the two events that actually scared him. He knew Holly would not hesitate to attack most anything if threatened, yet whatever she saw, she backed away from. So Ed wonders to this day, what could have been so frightening that Holly would seek protection? Holly would have instantly gotten between us and an angry bear and given her life, so what could be so frightening to this courageous canine?

I loved Holly, but animals are aware of spirits, especially if those spirits are malevolent, so although Holly provided certain protection, she also gave me chills many times during the day. It just was not unusual for Holly to look out into the apartment beyond the kitchen and give a low growl. She was letting me know something she regarded as a threat was out there. To go to the bathroom, I had to cross that threshold and many times, I would take Holly with me.

I can't absolutely say whether in these cases if Holly was a blessing, or would ignorance have been bliss? Looking back, although Holly would be present when much of the kitchen activity would take place, she rarely became defensive. If the cabinet door opened, she would just stare in that direction and never seemed threatened.

Dave was doing everything he could to make Ellen happy with no success. He completely disregarded her plea to move out. In retrospect, she gave him no substantial reason, as whatever was tormenting her was kept as her secret. All I ever knew was that when we shared time, she seemed happy. So it was with great surprise that in late June, Dave returned home to find Ellen packing.

"Where are you going?" he asked.

"I am taking a job as a nanny and leaving you."

Ellen made the statement emotionless, which left Dave in shock. One has to understand that Dave is a gentle and emotional man, and his only concern was for Ellen and his baby.

Apparently on her own, she found a place that needed a nanny and secured a live-in job. The job was far outside Chicago, and she intended to start immediately. She was leaving and taking the baby and Dave was completely blindsided by this. He was totally confused. Was it him? Was it living in the city? Was it the landlords? Was it the spirit activity that he accepted without fear? His mind just could not process what was happening or why.

He did everything he could to communicate, but Ellen remained silent and went about gathering everything that was hers, as far as personal items and all the baby's things. He watched and sat in complete shock. It was tear-filled eyes that saw a cab in front of the building and Ellen loading it up, taking the baby and leaving. They were young and in love, so how could this happen?

He knew the immediate solution was to find another apartment, but with his work schedule, that would take time. He assumed that when she was settled, she would call. He asked himself, was she really leaving him, or the apartment? If it was the apartment, then what caused her to leave with such urgency, not taking his feelings into account?

If it was him...why? Their arguments were minor. If the many hours he worked or his travel were issues, it had never surfaced. He never felt so helpless and alone. To this very day, he cannot wrap his head around this event. In talking with him some 42 years later, I can still sense the confusion. He was blindsided and had no clue why she was so anxious to leave. This remains the source of very sensitive and emotional memories.

It was days of not seeing Ellen before I went downstairs to knock on her door. Of course, no one answered. At first, I thought she might have gone shopping, so I tried later in the day with the same result. I was a bit worried that maybe the baby had become ill and they were at the hospital. I knew the odd hours Dave could work and that he was also known to travel and be away for days, so I continued to check downstairs or wait for a phone call. It was the next evening when I saw Dave and asked about Ellen. He put on a happy face and replied, "Oh, she went to visit her mother." He quickly opened his front door and was gone. I thought it strange, as he avoided any conversation.

You can imagine what went through my mind. It was not like Ellen not to have mentioned it in conversation, nor would she have not said goodbye, so I worried. She had never even talked about her mother. I knew something was wrong, but also knew it was none of my business. Instantly, I felt alone once again, knowing I would now return to my fortress in the kitchen with no one to talk with and no escape. I was, once again, isolated. I mentioned it to Ed, but he shrugged it off. With tenants, it was really none of our business. He was correct, except he did not know how close we had become and I was reluctant to tell him of the bond between Ellen and me.

Dave spent the next week in depression. He had no clue that Ellen was leaving or even why. His apartment became a very lonely place. Even more depressing was that Ellen seldom even called. Dave was confused and could not reason the source of his situation. He made a good living, and they had most of whatever they needed or wanted, so it could not be that. Like all young married couples, they had their minor spats, but nothing that would cause this.

He tried to occupy himself with his work, which was the only way he could maintain his composure. His world suddenly became very empty and he tried to come back to the apartment only to sleep. In his words, "the bedroom became a very lonely place." It was a short time after Ellen left that he awoke one morning to find tiny bites on his legs from the knee down. They were red and obviously new and agitated. It made no sense, as this was the room they slept in since moving in. His only logical thought was this was also the bedroom that their dog had slept in, so Dave imagined it was possibly fleas, although he found no fleas or signs of any.

He bought some flea powder and applied a salve to his legs and thought nothing of it. He treated the bed and carpet and then went to sleep the next night, after a long day. The next morning was the same, and he had countless new bites on his leg. He was totally baffled and wondered what kind of insect could he not see that would only bite him on his lower legs? Once again, he visited the store and bought every kind of powder and spray available. Back at home, he checked everything, only to find no sign of any type of insect. He blasted the room with sprays and powders. He sprayed the mattress and put on new sheets. He felt confident that this would solve the problem.

The following night he slept soundly, but upon awakening he was shocked that his legs were now covered in new bites. Dave was at a complete loss. Never did he and Ellen have a bug problem, plus he could find no sign of a flea or anything else. His legs were irritated and itching, so he only saw one solution and that was to sleep elsewhere. Dave did not like the first bedroom, which just seemed 'dark in a bad way,' so he moved the bed into the back bedroom, which he was now using as a workshop. Although it was off the back porch and had a feeling of poor ventilation, he hoped his 'bite' problem was over. Today, Dave understands there was no problem with ventilation, only that the air in that room was 'heavy.'

It was now July and hot and humid, but Dave did not mind the heat and what he thought was a lack of ventilation, as the room was dark and he enjoyed sleeping in a darker room. After his very first night sleeping in that room, he awoke fully rested and immediately checked his legs. Almost miraculously, they not only didn't have any new bites, but most of the old ones were healed and gone. Never did he think anything more than what he saw on the surface. He was satisfied sleeping in the back bedroom, and bought a folding bed to use, putting the big bed back so he was ready if Ellen returned. No way did he think Ellen would be gone for very long. He lived every day at this point thinking she and the baby would soon be walking through the front door.

Aside from the 'heavy' air, the first thing he experienced in the back bedroom was the strange scent of perfume, and it was not Ellen's. The scent was very strong at times and it was very different from Ellen's. His immediately thought was of the 'embrace' he felt at the bottom of the stairs on the back porch. Was it related? Was this the scent of the woman he had heard crying so many times?

Dave became conditioned to the scent and was not sure whether there was a tangible reason, or just his imagination. He began questioning his sanity at this point, because the scent was so foreign. It was soon after experiencing this unexplainable scent that he went to bed and was sleeping soundly and felt someone sleeping next to him. The first time it happened, he wanted to believe that Ellen returned and was lying next to him, but when he awoke, there was no one there. In his true Native belief, the event was not negative, so if it was a spirit, it was comforting. He had no fear.

Dave quickly became used to feeling someone sleeping beside him. In his mind, looking back, his loneliness made it a comfort. You must understand the native beliefs, because in Dave's mind, he was suffering from loneliness and interpreted this as a positive thing that he was made to feel like he was not alone. The one thing that continued and concerned him was the radiant heat from the oven on the stove. He knew the stove was not being used so, why was the oven door warm? He checked the pilot light and all appeared normal, so it remained a mystery.

Dave became used to coming home, smelling the scent of this sweet perfume, and lying in bed to feel someone or something beside him. Then, it took a turn that was very strange. One night, the spirit moved from being next to him, to moving on top of him. It was not erotic in any way and his instincts told him she wanted comfort. Given his Native beliefs, she did not harm or scare him, so he believed it was a kind spirit. He allowed this for days and maybe his loneliness contributed to him allowing this, but soon he began to put things together and took a different view. Could it be that this spirit, which he believed was the one he had previously heard crying and arguing, is caring for him? Did she attach herself to him? Was the warm stove a sign that she was cooking for him in the only way she could?

He reasoned that she knew he would not enter the first 'dark' bedroom, and maybe the bites were her way of driving him into that back bedroom. We were now in August, and he realized, though the air in that room was 'heavy,' that the temperature was always cool while he slept. There was another factor within the Native beliefs that came to his mind, and that was an evil spirit might disguise itself to gain one's confidence before revealing its true nature. He decided to abandon the back bedroom and begin sleeping on the couch in the living room.

He knew almost immediately that 'she' was unhappy with him abandoning that bedroom. The noises within the apartment became more frequent and louder. The dining room chandelier seemed like it never stopped swaying, and for the first time, he could hear noises in the basement. Initially, again, he would blame Ed, but he would soon find out otherwise. In his Native thinking, the spirit never harmed him, so he questioned whether he was doing the right thing.

He only spent a few nights sleeping on the couch until he was awakened by the sound of someone at the front door, only a few feet away. His first hope was that it was Ellen returning home, but when the sound continued, he became alert. He studied the sound and it was like someone attempting to 'pick' his lock. Again, his first thought was that it was Ed. Dave remembered that Ed mentioned he had worked for a locksmith while going to school, and knew how to use a pick set.

Dave forgot that we had keys to his apartment in case of an emergency, so Ed had no reason to pick his lock. Dave quietly walked to the door and opened it quickly, finding nothing there. He tried to interpret, 'why?' Was this a new visitor, or a warning of some kind?

During this period, we never realized Ellen was not at her mother's. Dave approached Ed telling him of the noises in the hall. Ed wondered if a member of Myra's family had kept or made a copy of the key to the outside entry door, so having knowledge of locks, Ed bought what is called a 'Chicago' lock. It was a door lock with a round key like those on vending machines. Ed was confident it could not be 'picked,' and it was registered, so no duplicate keys could be made. Ed thought this satisfied Dave, but he was unaware of the true nature of Dave's problems. In fact, Ed was paranoid of Myra's family and would have bet that it was they who were attempting to get back into the building to do some treasure hunting.

Ed was working as many hours as he could with the goal of paying our debts and saving money so that we could leave this place. During this period, I felt so alone. I was walking on eggshells, always examining every-thing, anticipating a 'happening.' That is one of the most significant effects of a haunting…it perpetually keeps you on edge. I was coming apart. I had the baby at my side at all times, but sitting in the kitchen watching the lit-tle TV became like being in prison. I don't remember the exact day of the week, but I decided to take my bath. I could only do this in the afternoons, after the baby was fed and was put down for her nap.

I filled the bathtub and looked forward to a few soothing minutes. I always left the bathroom door open so I could hear if the baby stirred. I sat in the hot water and relaxed for a few moments, but I had this strange feel-ing I was being watched. Being watched was a feeling I frequently had, but this was different. I felt it was close by. My immediate thought was it was only because I was naked and vulnerable. I felt a bit of urgency to finish, so I stepped out of the tub and began to dry off when I felt this chill, like there was someone standing behind me.

As I turned to make sure the door was still open, I felt a hand grasp my shoulder. It was a very large hand and ever so cold, and I knew it was not Ed. I did not scream, but I pulled away quickly and turned to see nothing, but I knew something was definitely there. Right before my eyes, the bath-room door closed. It was an immediate panic, as I imagined I was locked in. I don't think there is a way to describe what flashed through my head. Just for a second, I felt totally trapped. All that goes through a mother's thoughts are about the baby! It was a great relief that the door opened as normal, and after checking that the baby was still asleep, I called Ed. I was hysterical.

He explained that there was no way he could leave his job, so he would see me when he arrived home. I had hit my limits. I kept thinking that a dead guy grabbed me! I became completely paranoid, knowing that I could be touched. I felt he could do it again at any time. Now, I was in real fear. Erase all the Hollywood images created in the last 45 years, and you have nothing to imagine but the image of a dead man, and that is what I lived with.

From that moment on, I was completely paranoid. If something brushed against me, I would have a tinge of fear and pull away quickly. If I heard a foreign sound, I jumped. I held onto this image of a dead, old pervert reaching out at me. Even worse, the only image my mind could produce was that which resembled what an old man would look like, coming out of a casket. I could never forget that cold hand grasping my shoulder.

I desperately needed a break and to get away from all this. I needed one night of normal sleep without waking at every sound or having nightmares. I just wanted to go home. I wanted to sleep in my old childhood bedroom without a care. I desperately wanted to talk and be with my mom, who I hoped would understand and maybe even offer some advice. Ellen was still gone, but knowing she went to see her mom, I came to the conclusion that I should do the same. My big mental obstacle was...how do I break this to Ed?

Although he admitted that we were dealing with something we could not control, it was almost like he had blinders on. By now, I was conditioned to keeping many of these happenings to myself. This one I could not contain. I had been touched! And, I knew it was the large hand of a dead man! I just wanted to leave. I had to ask Ed if I could get away long enough to get my mental strength back.

I sat in my kitchen and was trying to figure out how I could ask Ed to go home for awhile. I was torn, because we had never been apart, and it made me feel selfish that I wanted to escape and was leaving him here alone. I decided I would ask him at dinner. I still remember that evening. He was tired from a long day, as usual, and I knew he was mentally planning to work on the building and do who knows what in the endless list of repairs and painting. All that was on my mind was asking this big question and predicting his response and how I might react. He had stopped asking about my days long ago, because he already knew my answers...or he did not want to know, because he could do nothing about it.

When he was about finished eating, I popped the question.

"Eddie, I want to go home for awhile."

He just stared at me with no response, so I continued.

"I need a break. I just can't take it anymore."

His eyes told me his feelings. "Are you leaving me?" he asked softly.

"No! I just want to get away and get my head together. If I stay here, I am going to lose my mind. I just need a break."

"How long?" he asked.

"I don't really know. It will be as long as I need."

He was silent for a few minutes, but it seemed much longer. I expected him to get angry. Instead, he looked at me and stated, "All we have is enough for a one way ticket if we are lucky, but depending how long you stay, I can send you the money to return. Go ahead; make the plane reservation."

Ed got up and put on his work clothes and headed out to the garage. I felt terrible, because his reaction was only of sadness and an argument would have made things much easier. I called the airline and at the time, there were three flights to Tulsa a day. I booked one for the next evening.

These were much different times. Airlines were competing and the flights left like clockwork, regardless of the number of passengers. Passengers were actually treated as special for choosing to fly, as opposed to riding the train or driving. Remember, gas was only 30 cents a gallon!

It was a pleasure to fly in 1971. People today cannot even imagine how the flying experience has deteriorated.

I began packing. As bad as I felt about leaving Ed alone, I was also excited that I would get away from all this activity. At least nothing could touch me. Ed made it worse, because he accepted my request without debate. I knew he knew that this was necessary for me to maintain my sanity. I don't really know how Ed kept himself together and whether it was logic, rationalizing, courage, or denial, but I knew he was facing this head on without a trace of fear. Because he never spoke of any personal incidents, I almost thought that the ghosts might be avoiding him. Of course, they were not avoiding him, but he viewed them as an adversary and he just didn't like to lose. At bedtime, there was no major discussion and we fell asleep holding each other, as usual.

The next morning was a bit uncomfortable, as I was feeling guilty about leaving, but we discussed it without emotion. We agreed that I would stay until I felt strong enough to return. It was easy to pass the time away knowing I was leaving. Nothing bothered me that day, as all I could think about was seeing my mom and dad and my little sister. I wanted to talk with my mom and I hoped she might have answers or suggestions regarding our situation. Ed returned home, and we were on our way to O'Hare International airport. The airport was much smaller in 1971 and parking was literally next to the terminal. In a few years it would become the world's busiest airport…but not today. A passionate kiss goodbye and I was on my way. I was torn and sad and I felt very selfish as the plane took off. I could see Ed waving goodbye through the terminal window.

It was only an hour and a half and we were landing in Tulsa. It was such a great feeling, seeing my parents smiling at the gate. We drove home and I quickly unpacked and made myself and the baby comfortable. I knew my dad had no clue as to why I was there, and maybe thought our marriage was in trouble, so I let him know that this was not the case. I was waiting until the next day so I could go one-on-one with my mom, regarding our problems. No one but a haunting survivor could imagine the feeling of living your life without the anxiety of anticipating unexpected activity. I slept like a baby, and longer than I had in months.

My little sister and my mom jumped at the chance of caring for Christine, so it really became a vacation. Getting up at 7:00 a.m. was a treat from being up at 4:30 a.m., as was my usual. It was time enough to say goodbye to dad before he left for work, and to help see my sister off to school. Finally, I had my mom alone. Mom knew I had a problem, and likely thought it was my marriage, but after we made a fresh cup of coffee and the baby was fed and napping, we sat down to talk.

The least I expected was coffee and sympathy, and hoped that maybe my mother knew something that might help our situation. When I told her about our problem and the activity, she just smirked. In a way that I was very familiar with, she sent me the signal that my conversation was absurd. She didn't offer anything, but half-listened to me before completely changing the subject, as if I never brought it up. I recognized that she was treating me like a little girl that just had a bad dream. She literally refused to discuss it.

After opening up and presenting my problems and fears and asking for direction, she simply ignored me and asked, "Change the channel dear," as if everything I had said had fallen on deaf ears.

I was crushed. I sat there, knowing my mother was thinking that either I was imagining these things or worse yet, that I was a liar. It was no different than what Ed and I had experienced with others, but somehow much more hurtful coming from my mother. This was typical of bringing up this subject matter in 1971. Now, when my mom looked at me, I wondered if she was thinking that I had lost my mind. I became embarrassed that I even had brought the subject up in the first place. I knew my trip to Tulsa may give me a good night's sleep, but there was no emotional comfort to be had. At this moment, I felt foolish even making the trip and wished Ed would come and get me.

People often ask why True Haunting was not published until 40 years later and why Ed wanted it published in our daughter's name. This was why. Most everyone we attempted to talk with considered us crazy, or over exercising our imaginations. I learned quickly not to bring this up to the rest of my family. The truth is that most of our friends and family first learned of our story when they read the book, True Haunting.

It was about three days before Ed called. Understand that long distance calls were operator assisted and very expensive. I tried my best to project that all was well and the trip was worthwhile, but I knew he sensed otherwise because he kept asking, "What's the matter?" If you have read True Haunting, you will understand that Ed was getting a number of experiences that were new to him. I should have known that without me there, they might unleash their energy in his direction…and they did. He never mentioned anything, so I would later learn about some new games they were playing. I didn't ask to come home yet and we ended the call without an agreement as to when I would return.

On the first floor, Dave was enduring more activity and noise. He avoided the back bedroom and workshop and gradually the scent of perfume was gone. Knowing I was away and Ed was at work, Dave would hear sounds coming from our apartment. Usually it was like furniture being moved about, to the extent that at times he actually felt maybe our apartment was being vandalized. Dave absolutely knew the building had more than one spirit and they were certainly active, but felt no sign there was anything as dark as he was taught, regarding an evil spirit. He did decide good, bad, or otherwise, that he would not interact or entertain them in any way. Dave would pray in his Native way that these spirits would find peace and move elsewhere.

It was the week Marsha was gone that Dave received a phone call. It was from Ellen's employer. He coldly asked for Dave to pick up his baby and their belongings and was told that Ellen was at the local hospital in the Emergency Room. He immediately drove to the house and picked up his child and belongings and proceeded to the hospital. Ellen was eventually released. The reason for the hospitalization remains personal. After finding out Ellen would be okay, Dave was happy to have his family back, but Ellen showed no signs of being happy to return.

Dave quickly realized Ellen was changed. She was not her bubbly smiling self, but serious and withdrawn. He tried everything he could to make her feel better, but she remained in a depressed state. There was no doubt in his mind that Ellen did not want to return home. There was a distance between them that he did not understand, and frankly, did not know how to overcome. He was just confused by the whole situation. Dave decided not to force the issue, so when they returned home, he let Ellen know that he would sleep on the couch. When she did not object, he was plagued with guilt; confused by what he might have done to create this distance.

They spent the evening watching TV, with Dave overjoyed at having his daughter in his arms once again. Somehow, he had to find out from Ellen if their marriage had any future, but in her state of mind, he was reluctant to do so anticipating the worst possible answer. When it was time for bed, Ellen went to their bedroom and Dave wondered if she would experience the flea bites. He hoped Ellen would ask him to come to bed, but she didn't, so he slept on the couch. The next morning, Ellen awoke rested and without flea bites. He never mentioned it to her, and she likely wondered why he kept staring at her legs.

With Dave going to work, the first thing Ellen did was come upstairs to talk with me, but found no one there. That evening, she waited for Ed to ask where I was. He explained that I went to visit my mother in Tulsa. Ellen certainly had an understanding as to why. The only thing Ed immediately noticed was Ellen was void of her smile, and she had dark circles around her eyes, as if she hadn't slept for days. Ed immediately knew this was not the same Ellen.

We actually can't remember exactly, but it was no more than a week or so before Ed called and I asked to come home. I enjoyed seeing my parents and they worked so hard to give me a great time, but I had the empty feeling that I left Ed stranded. Plus, I knew there was no mental comfort to be had. I kept it all in so much that my stepfather never knew this story until he read True Haunting. Certain evenings I would sit and watch them watching the TV without a care and wish that could be Ed and I. I wondered if that day would ever come again.

Ed explained we did not have money for a return flight and I was not about to ask my parents, as I was too embarrassed. Ed could hear it in my voice and knew something was wrong. He decided to work the next day and afterward drive through the night to come get me. I agreed.

When he arrived, I wished we could all just stay there in Tulsa and not leave. I was not looking forward to returning to that apartment. I could not rid myself of the fact that a dead man had touched me. It was on that drive home that Ed finally acknowledged our problem. Apparently, he had a number of experiences and one was that they had turned on the stove. He decided we would take any means available to try and 'clean' this building. For the first time, he talked of approaching other Christian denominations and even going beyond to rid us of these ghosts. He had no knowledge of psychics or gifted people or that they even existed, so his possible solutions were aimed at various religious denominations. This, despite that it was considered a sacrilege to do so within the Catholic faith, at that time.

When we returned home, we talked as I put the baby down and unpacked. It was not unusual that we heard footsteps coming from the back porch stairs. Ed went to investigate and eventually, returned with Holly. My assumption was that the footsteps were from Dave, bringing Holly back. Ed seemed a bit down, and after a bit of probing, informed me that Dave wants to move out and asked to be released from their lease. The reason was that while we were both away, the noise coming from our apartment was almost nightly and too much to take. This combined with the arguing and footsteps, pushed Dave to want to leave....or so he said.

We had no knowledge that his main motivation was with Ellen, as she needed to leave and Dave wanted to save his marriage. Today, we know that none of the activity frightened Dave, and it was just an annoyance. My heart sank a bit, thinking that with Ellen being gone, I would once more be alone all day. I had no idea that Ed's sister, April, had already approached him to move in if our current tenants left.

I related my experience in Tulsa, and how my mother not only did not comfort me, but that she didn't even acknowledge our problem. The few nights sleep was a great relief, but other than that, my trip home was unrewarding and depressing. My family, had no comprehension of spirits or ghosts and more than that, they certainly didn't want any. Once that door of knowledge or experience is opened, it can never close, so in reality, ignorance is truly bliss.

After eating a quick sandwich, we went to sleep. We awoke as usual with coffee, and I shared more of my displeasure about my family. Ed then took his bath, dressed, and grabbed his attaché to leave. Then, a problem surfaced. His keys were gone from the hook where he always hung them, by the door. He began searching about, swearing and becoming angry. He explained that they had done this before when I was away.

At the top of the cabinet, he found his keys. I still remember him simply staring at them.

"What the hell is with this?" He showed me a key on the ring that was bent in an 'L' shape. "Why this key? It is the garage key. It is from a new lock and has nothing to do with this building." He showed me the key.

"Look at this closely; this bend has no stress cracks. It looks like this was done by heat...the bastards did this last week and threw them in the sink. What is up with the garage key? The damned garage is empty, so what is the message?"

The bent key baffled his logic, as the key was new and so was the lock. Neither item had an attachment to the house. He had no way to deny or rationalize this. The only humorous thing was that he went to sleep with the keys under his pillow that night!

It was the next weekend that we went to a nursing facility to see Ed's Aunt Helen. She had been fighting a losing battle with breast cancer for about five years. She was dying, and we did not know how close to death she actually was. This was Ed's favorite aunt, and they were close. She gave him serious advice after visiting us at the building the previous Christmas. She handed him a new book, 'The Exorcist,' and told him to read it.

She then recommended strongly that we move out as soon as we could. I did feel that his Aunt Helen was special. Today, I would consider her to have been what some might refer to as a 'sensitive.' She knew we had something dark in that building that might be dangerous. Fortunately, neither of us read the book until a year or so later, or it would have scared us to death. His Aunt Helen passed a few days later.

We returned home to find Holly all excited and manically moving about the kitchen. Immediately, I began calling out for my cat, Kitty. With no response, we began searching the house frantically. I believe it was me that saw the open window in our bedroom, and then I became hysterical. It was only open about a foot, but obvious, because we rarely ever opened it. Looking straight down from the window, on the concrete, was Kitty. Although I called out, she remained motionless. Ed ran down the stairs and the next thing I knew, he was bringing her into the apartment. She was completely unharmed. It seemed impossible. In fact, it was impossible. How this overweight, declawed house cat could fall 20 feet onto concrete and wind up without a scratch was more than a miracle. All I remember was Ed, calculating the distance and shaking his head.

"There is no way she could have fallen over 20 feet onto cement and not broken anything, much less survived," he stated. "The sons-a-bitches must have floated her down! No way was that window open, and I know that for a fact. They could have killed her, but they didn't. This makes no sense, other than sending us some kind of message. Look at her! Not a hair out of place! That is fucking impossible." [***His language, not mine.***]

It took us hours to shake off the feeling that we were being threatened. Our conclusion was that it was time to urgently seek some kind of help. Today, one can easily go to a website specializing in ghostly investigations, or reach out to the Order of Exorcists, who will send a qualified member of the clergy to help. But this was 1971, and we had no resources. We knew that regardless of where we went, we were doomed to be laughed at, or called some form of crazy...but we had no other choice. We both understood that since we couldn't move out, we must find a way to resolve this problem.

So the search would begin.

CHAPTER FIVE

Where do we go for help now?

The ghosts were actively terrorizing our animals, so we should have anticipated what would come next, because when Ed let Holly out the next morning, she instantly ran the length of the backyard, jumped the back gate, and took off. All I heard was the standard, "Son-Of-A-Bitch!"

Ed took off running after her. To clarify the brevity of what Ed wrote in True Haunting, he chased after the dog and we did put an ad in the paper. He walked around outside that evening, hoping Holly would maybe get hungry and return...but she never did. We can only wonder if Holly realized she could be next to go out the window. Since we didn't talk with our tenants all that much, we never knew Dave and Ellen lost Stephanie or even that they ever had a dog until 42 years later. 42 years later I found it strange that Ellen had never mentioned it?

The next morning, before Ed left for work, I asked him; "Where do we start looking for help?"

Honestly, I didn't know if his answer was meant to be a joke or serious, but he responded, "Look through the yellow pages." Now, this was the exact words of a local commercial for the telephone company, but I took him seriously.

I already knew there would be no listings under 'ghosts,' so I looked up the only thing I was familiar with; 'fortune tellers.' The listings were all advertisements about palm readers, etc., and not what we needed. Somehow, I drifted into psychics. To my surprise, under 'psychic services' were two listings. I did not hesitate in calling the first one. I was greeted by the warm voice of a woman. I fumbled for my words as I asked for help. It was a pretty long conversation and she stated her group would come to us that very evening and help us with the problem. She sounded very, very confident. I, of course, was overjoyed.

It was not long before Ellen was at the door. There was no mention of where she had gone or why, other than staying with Dave's story that she was at her mother's house. I noticed right off that she was not herself. She had dark circles around her eyes and her smile had faded. I gave her as many opportunities to talk about it as I could, but she didn't. There was no sign that she wanted to move, much less leave Dave. I was in an upbeat mood, knowing that help was possibly on the way, which I shared with her.

She asked that whatever these people were going to do, would they also do the same to her apartment. I told her I would get it done for sure, and to be ready because I was not sure how many people there would be, but I did know that they would inspect her apartment. I was excited and optimistic. When Ed returned home, I announced what I had done and he was shocked, but slightly pessimistic. Growing up in Chicago made him leery of scams. His first question was, "How much do they want?"

"Free! These people do this for free."

"Where did you find them?" he wondered.

"I found them in the yellow pages. They were listed in the phone book."

I expected a smile, but instead he just shook his head. "Okay."

It was after a quick dinner that our doorbell rang. It was two men and two women. The men were carrying a piece of equipment which I later learned was a type of tape recorder. If you read True Haunting, you will see that mine and Ed's perspectives differ. I saw four caring people, while Ed saw one possibly gifted person and three idiots. True Haunting tells the story, but I met two gifted women and two caring men. They took their time going through the house and both women were stunned by what they felt in the first bedroom on the first floor. They spent more time in and around that room than any place in the building. That is what Dave considered the 'dark' room. The women agreed that something very bad and very strong dominated that room. [*As it turned out, this is the same room the exorcist and psychic would focus on*] Oddly, although they opened the basement door from the first floor apartment, they did not go into the basement. All I caught was the concerned look that they gave each other.

It made me wonder if they had felt what I felt about that basement. There was something about it that was forbidding. After about a half hour or so we all returned upstairs to our kitchen. They suggested a ritual and lit candles, and asked for us to all hold hands. Some prayers were then said and although the tape recorder was running, they made no attempt to play anything back. During the prayers, the closed kitchen door opened, as Ed had never tied it. This caused one of the men who had a bright red toupee to get very nervous. They all became obviously nervous when the kitchen lights flickered.

It was apparent our ghosts had no respect for these people and were letting them know they were certainly there! I watched as Ed looked amused, and the man in the red wig began sweating and constantly looking behind, as if a monster would be popping up. The stout man addressed the spirits in what he thought was a commanding voice. Myself? I did not hear the confidence. He told them to leave and that they did not belong here. In the Lord's name, he commanded, "Be gone!"

The other man announced that now the house was clean. Ed was looking at them as if they were absolute morons. The man in the red wig could not pack things up fast enough, and as he packed, he looked nervously around. They moved toward the exit door, and as they did, I saw the man in the red wig's eyes become wide; then I heard the clunk behind me, and knew he had seen the phone rise off the hook. With that, they hurried out. Ed was standing with his mouth open. I was sure he wasn't positive whether to laugh or be pissed.

"What the hell was that? Give me a break! Be gone?" Ed asked.

"I have no idea..." I replied.

"Now we have no problem, they say? They couldn't get their asses out of here fast enough. Did you see that guy in the red wig? His hair went crooked. Man, is he in the wrong business. Did you see how fast that guy ran down the stairs? He flew faster than Father Barnes!"

We both agreed that the one woman was psychic, and she seemed to sense many things about the house accurately, especially the 'dark' bedroom. I felt my heart drop, as I had high hopes. I wasn't sure what these people were looking for, but here it was and they scurried out. I still had the other listing up my sleeve, so I clung to it as a shred of hope.

Ellen and Dave came up and within minutes, Ed had us all laughing. He noticed the guy in the red wig resembled Don Knotts from Mayberry. We argued a bit over their abilities, because Ed admitted the one woman was somehow different from the rest, but I thought both were psychic and had abilities. We all agreed that the men were curiosity seekers at best, and not emotionally suited for confronting ghosts.

"I have another group to call," I brought up. "They are listed as psychic research."

We bantered and joked for an hour or so and called it a night. I watched Ellen. She seemed removed from the whole moment, as if her mind was wandering. I began to wonder, for the first time, if Ellen had more serious problems than she let on to. Both of the women agreed that the darkest room was the first bedroom on the first floor under the stairs. Ellen clearly heard them and did not make any comments. Was whatever in that room tormenting her? Was that what she was running away from? If so, why didn't she tell Dave? Even if she considered him to be superstitious, he would likely react as any loving husband would; with concern, I would think.

For the rest of the night all Ed did was ridicule the group. He could not believe how they could solicit ghostly events and have so much fear. He labeled them as scammers. He figured they visit 'clean' homes, selling the occupants a false bill of goods and maybe even charge for their service at some point. Charge or not, they certainly appeared as charlatans facing the real thing.

My hopes were dashed, but I still held out some hope for the second group. My only fear was that if this second group was a fraud, where do I go from there?

I could hardly wait to call the second number in the phone book. Right from the beginning, they sounded more professional, as a secretary answered the phone. She took down my information in a very businesslike manner, with a number of specific questions, and assured me that someone would soon be in touch. I felt slightly depressed, as there seemed to be no real sense of urgency. Still, I held out hope.

As usual, Ellen joined me for coffee. Strangely, once again, never was there any talk about her visit to her mother's, which I thought was a bit weird. I did tell her about my visit and how returning home just wasn't the same. She was not the Ellen that I knew, for she was withdrawn and serious. I probed a bit, thinking there was trouble with their marriage, but she never gave me a hint. The deep, dark, circles under her eyes, were a giveaway that she was not sleeping well. I told her about my call to a second psychic group, and of my hopes that they would come to the rescue. It was that morning that it seemed Ellen could not hold it all in any longer. She began relating various activity and her fears which included moving her baby away from the 'dark' room. I'm sure she did not tell me everything, but the moving chandelier, the power interruptions, the constant noise above their heads, the footsteps, arguing, and the constant opening of the basement door was getting to her. She did feel that their baby was well aware of an entity within their apartment. Although she said she was not afraid, I sensed she definitely was. She did warn me not to speak with Dave about the activity. It was not like Dave was unaware, because he seemed to have his suspicions already and even more than we ever knew.

I believe it was during this 'waiting for help' period that we decided to go to the local library. It was nice to get out of the apartment, but the trip yielded nothing. There were plenty of ghost stories of mainly fiction, but nothing that we would consider in paranormal education. What we needed was, "Ghosts for Dummies," which didn't exist. So we would wait for the second wave of help.

It was that weekend that Dave had another strange experience. It was a Sunday and we went out to visit Ed's mother. Ellen had taken the baby and went shopping, leaving Dave on his own. Dave was hearing noises above him and assumed we were home. He went to the kitchen and could hear children in the basement, which was unusual. He opened the door and walked down a few stairs to capture a glance, and he saw two little girls running around and playing. They were both wearing white dresses. He watched as they ran about the basement chasing one another, as children do.

He came down the stairs a bit further, looking for an adult, as he knew it would not be like us to leave children to play in that basement alone. All he saw were the little girls, and he figured they must be visiting, and belonged to us. He watched for about 10 minutes and their play seemed harmless, so he went back to his apartment and continued his day. He would find out later in the day that we were not at home. He never doubted what he witnessed, but was only confused at what was the meaning. As was his Native beliefs, he was stunned, but in the end, he realized he had only seen what he interpreted as two happy spirits.

His only amazement was that they were as solid as you or I. It was an event that he would keep to himself until 42 years later when he confided in us. Ed and I could not make sense of it, since we never had any indication of children in our experience having been in the Campbell Street building. Yet Dave described their exact appearance and movement.

However, if you watch the original NBC news footage on YouTube [True Haunting] you will see at the 1.40 minute mark, something white, which seems to approach the dark doorway on the left and then back off. It was never noticed, except by a reader who wrote us and asked the question as to what it was. Marsha and I had seen apparitions, but never anything white, so we made no sense of it. Since all of us were behind the camera and that bedroom had no door, we now know that we captured a trace of a ghost. Now, with Dave's little girls in white dresses story, it made some sense in seeing this solid white anomaly.

It was Monday, and I received a phone call that a representative would be stopping by to interview us that evening. He sounded so serious and businesslike, that I became a bit unsure of what direction this might take. An interview? I was puzzled, because I had hoped it would be someone to take some action, but I agreed. When Ed arrived home, all he had were questions.

"Who is this guy?"

"Who does he represent?"

"What the hell kind of interview is this?"

"If he has a contract and asks for money, I'm kicking his ass out!"

Ed wasn't happy and didn't understand why we were being interviewed. After dinner, precisely at 7 PM, our doorbell rang. It was a man named Tom Valentine. He was older than us, but looked younger than his age. There was a boyish innocence that he projected that put us at ease immediately. I think Ed imagined someone looking more like an interrogator. We invited him in and he quickly made us feel comfortable, as I guess this is a talent all good reporters must have. This would later make sense, as Tom originally was a reporter for an LA paper. He was now an author, having written, "Psychic Mission," a book about the life of psychic Joseph DeLouise. The actual purpose of the interview was to be sure that this was an authentic case. For a psychic, the media was not kind and they had to be sure we were not setting Joseph up to be debunked. Plus, they needed to know whether our situation warranted their attention. We would learn more, but for now, he took out his notebook and pen and began firing questions at us.

"How old are you?"

"Is this your first child?"

"How long have you been married?"

"What are your religious beliefs?"

"Do you get along?"

"Do you drink or do drugs?"

"What is your education?"

The questions seemed endless.

He wanted to know everything and more, and I watched Ed bristle and hesitate as Tom asked questions regarding our personal habits. He wanted to know about our family, where Ed worked, his occupation, even our daily habits. He asked if he could investigate the apartment and went about writing and taking notes, even looking in our refrigerator.

Finally, Tom asked about the activity we were experiencing. For every activity we listed, he had a dozen questions. When he finished, the roles reversed, as Ed began asking the questions. The most interesting of which was how Tom went from being a newspaper reporter with LA's top paper, to being involved with investigating the unknown. The story he told us is well worth relating and a warning to those not to dabble in the occult.

Tom had taken an assignment doing a feature report on mental illness. As a true analyst, he visited a mental institution. There, he took the patient records, dividing them by diagnosis, age, etc.. Remember, this was in a day long before computers, so he was knee deep in paperwork and files. In doing this, one category puzzled him; there was a group of patients that had no previous record of mental illness, no traumatic events, no chemical imbalances, no evidence of drug use...but evidence of occult-like participation. He studied these cases out of curiosity.

What became obvious was that séances, dark arts, Ouija boards, and such seemed to be a common thread that ran through a significant sized group of patients. The symptoms that caused them to be institutionalized were paranoia, being terrorized, violence, depression, and even a total loss of identity. What he found was so compelling, that it redirected his life into the paranormal. So he quit a lucrative full time job of writing a column, and literally stepped into the unknown. He met Joseph DeLouise, a psychic, when Joe was working with the LA police, and helped locate Tex Watson, a Manson family member. Joseph had gained notoriety by making a number of accurate predictions, including a major bridge collapse. This resulted in Tom linking with Joseph and authoring the book, Psychic Mission. Now, we assumed he was working with this research group and likely gathering facts for another possible book. The one thing we both felt, was that Tom cared. In the end, he reflected a genuine concern for our overall well being.

Tom left us, only telling us that he would be 'in-touch.' What did that mean? We would soon find out, because about three days later he called for a second interview. It was our guess that he spent the time fact-checking the information he collected on his first visit. When he arrived for the second visit, it was much more casual. This time, he met with our first floor tenants that likely shared little, from what we assumed. He explained that one, if not two psychics would be visiting, and they would need full access to the building, including the basement, attic, and garage. He explained that they would attempt to define what we had in the building and how to possibly get rid of it.

At this point, I saw Tom as our knight in shining armor, as it sounded as if he was bringing qualified people to our rescue. I could tell Ed liked Tom, but was still a bit skeptical as to how all this was going to work, plus his 'Chicago' mentality was anticipating a bill for their services. He left us with only the promise that someone will be calling us soon.

I shared this with Ellen, as I had to prepare her for whomever it was that would need to investigate their apartment. She seemed excited that we were going to get some help. I never knew how much she counted on this to be successful, as she never shared her true torment. What was bothering her was her secret that she never even shared with her husband.

I desperately wanted whatever was here to be gone. After being touched, I could not erase that from my mind. I was constantly wondering if I was being watched. It caused me to do everything that was personal a lot quicker. I would bathe quickly, always when Ed was home. I would also dress quickly, always wondering if he was there near me, watching me. There is no way to describe my feelings of fear and paranoia. I had been violated. Is there any way I can properly describe something that can touch you at will but can never be seen?

It was a Friday when I received a call that Joseph DeLouise would be visiting. I knew of the book, but I had no real knowledge of who he was or even what he did. Ed and I were both anxiously waiting. It was like this man might wave a wand and our troubles would be over. When the doorbell rang, Ed rushed down the stairs. However, when Ed led them up the stairs, I saw the skeptical look on his face. In came Joseph, Tom, and a female protégé that we only met once. Both Joseph and his protégé looked mysterious. They were both dressed in black, both had black hair, and Joseph had a goatee. I could see Ed's eyebrow was raised.

Joseph had made some comments and was likely just talking out loud, but Ed felt he was pointing out the obvious to him. It was when they entered the kitchen that the woman grabbed Ed's hand. She looked him in the eyes and stated, 'bullets.'

I had no idea what the hell she was talking about. To my surprise, Ed countered, "Where?"

"In the basement," she replied. "Above the rafter."

I saw the look of astonishment on Ed's face and only later did he explain what the whole exchange meant to him. He had found a jar with bullets in it and hid it in the basement rafters. At that point, I watched Ed relax and hand over all the keys. He explained that Dave and Ellen were prepared for them to investigate their apartment. Ed had the ladder on the back porch set so they could look in the attic, and basement door and garage were left unlocked.

This would be a very revealing evening, but initially it began silently as they made few comments we could only hear from a distance and went about examining the building and various rooms. We sat in the kitchen, anticipating a possible solution. Most honestly, we had no idea of what to expect. In our best projection, we hoped they would just say "be gone!" and it would be over. In 1971, we had no reference for how these things were done or what to look forward to.

Author, Tom Valentine & Psychic Joseph DeLouise, 1971.

93

They were roaming for hours before they returned to the kitchen and gave us their opinion. They felt it was very serious. As the conversation proceeded, it was the first time I found out a bit about how much Ed knew and was keeping from me, and it was quite substantial. They estimated that we had at least five entities. One, for sure, was an old woman, and two were definitely men, with at least two undefined. The protégé explained that a woman had committed suicide in the garage. At that point Ed interrupted and stated, "I was told in the basement?"

Suicide? Ed knew? All I heard was a whirlwind of information flying across the table that I was never aware of. Also, that a young man had possibly died and was impaired either physically or mentally. Given that Ed had left some evidence from the 'collection' for them to see and handle, they described one as being evil and perverted. They attributed the arguing and crying we were all hearing was of the woman and the husband, and they claimed it was her that committed suicide. There was one spirit that was described as benign and even motherly, which we already knew and had seen. BUT, it became more serious when Joseph stated he could not define what was in the first floor bedroom, the so-called 'dark' room under the stairs.

Ed did a lot of talking, and it was then that I knew he was well aware of this family's history...or, at least, what he had learned from things he found in the building and from neighbors. It was also the first time Ed mentioned that he had found a well worn Ouija board in the house. Although Ed mentioned it casually, including the fact that he destroyed it, this brought about a serious mood. A well worn Ouija board in a house occupied only by adults meant that it was seriously used with purpose, and that purpose was to invite communication with something unknown.

This was a revelation and to Joseph, a significant factor. He explained the negative possibilities of using the Ouija. At this point, Joseph had to consider that it was possible that one of the entities was something the family actually invited in through the Ouija board. He did not elaborate, but we could see in his demeanor that there was an overcast of dread. One thing I remember is that Joseph thought our cat was 'special.' He offered to buy her and of course I refused. I think he sensed that Kitty could sniff these energies out.

Joseph said he would definitely help us, and needed some time to prepare. He left us only with the fact that he would be in touch. After they left, Ed had a lot to answer for and relate to me all he knew. Ed began talking, and I was amazed at what facts he had accumulated. Despite explaining some of the things we had talked about earlier, I still knew he was holding back, but he did tell me who the man was that stood on the other side of the street, staring at our building. It was the last remaining living son of the family that had built this building. He had a falling out with his family and moved out down the block, yet stood for a moment and stared at our building almost every single day.

I do regret that we never approached him to learn his story. Was he just stopping by to say hello to the spirits he knew were here? One disadvantage Joseph and Rev. Derl-Davis had, was neither, Dave or Ellen had been honest about all their activity, while Ed and I held back nothing. This was huge, as this would have made the first floor the focus of the cleansing instead of our apartment. At that time, we thought our apartment had the most significant activity, but it wasn't true. Had we known everything, I know Ed would have never let his sister move in and his book, True Haunting, would have had a much different ending.

Unknown to us, Joseph felt that whatever was in that 'dark' bedroom was more than he could handle. He felt it was demonic, but never said that word in our presence nor did he mention it might be a situation that was far beyond his capabilities as a medium. Joseph knew he definitely would need help and contacted Father Joseph Wood, a friend who also had a Catholic radio program on NBC. He wanted Father Wood's assistance, but he had to refuse, only because of the urgency that Joseph demanded.

As a Catholic priest, he had to abide by a strict protocol, which was a process that could take months, so Fr. Wood recommended Rev. William Derl-Davis, an actual exorcist. We had never heard that term before. What was an exorcist? We didn't know demons from doorknobs.

The only thing we can assume is that Father Joseph Wood somehow communicated to NBC that Joseph DeLouise was involved in helping us regarding our haunting. Fr. Wood knew that if Joseph was asking for his help, it had to be taken seriously. It was a complete surprise when Carole Simpson called. We had known her as the premier reporter at our local NBC TV station. She asked me if NBC could be involved and film whatever was taking place. I told her I had to talk it over with my husband, and she stated she would call back the next day.

When I asked Ed, he instantly refused. He was flat out against it, because he thought it would just result is us being ridiculed and labeled as being crazy, with our faces plastered all over the city. He imagined us going to public places and having people pointing and laughing at us.

We were then contacted by Tom Valentine, who asked us to allow NBC to do whatever coverage they wanted. He told Ed that it would be a favor to him and Joseph, since his book had just been released and he hoped it could be used as a promotion. Ed really was torn apart on this because on the one hand, he did not want to appear on TV and be labeled a nut case, but on the other, Joseph and Tom had asked for nothing and were helping us for free. In the end, Ed said okay.

When Carole Simpson called, I gave her our approval and she wanted us for a pre-interview, explaining that they would spend a day or two filming the house. It was a surprise, that two days of filming would go into what we were told to be a simple piece of news.

Being on the phone with Carole was like talking to a friend. Her interest was genuine and, as I learned, she had a very spiritual background, so this was a serious subject for her. I liked her immediately and Ed would eventually also, but for the initial period, he was paranoid that this reporter might make us look silly. He was well aware that these interviews could be edited to suit any purpose.

It was only a few days later that a huge NBC truck pulled up and a film crew arrived with Carole Simpson. We held the initial interview in our living room; you can imagine how much I cleaned house knowing the world might be looking in. There was only one cameraman and one sound man, and some huge lights. Both of us were nervous at first, but within minutes, Carole turned it into a personal discussion. We forgot about everything around us and were telling our story to an old friend. It was a magic that Carole had, as she put us at ease almost instantly.

What shocked Ed was that there were no silly questions; instead, it was handled like serious news. We were quite taken when a second truck pulled up with more cameras, and they began filming the house, inside and out. The interview ended, but the cables and cameras would be all over the house for two days. They shot 16 hours of film. 42 years later, we found that it was all lost in the NBC archives. Since the only footage is on YouTube as the "First Exorcism," or "True Haunting," and since it captured a ghost in the doorway at about the 1.40 minute mark, we can only wonder what else was captured in that 16 hours of lost film. The one thing we know for sure is that in 1971, no one was expecting or looking to capture anything ghostly.

When it was all over, Carole let us know that she would coordinate with Joseph and be here to film on the day of the exorcism. Ed found Carole to be sincere, and it surprised him that she displayed no skepticism and was so interested in our emotional well being. She gave me her personal phone number and even said to call her if I needed someone to talk with. It was clear that this was not just a report for Carole, and that she was concerned for our situation.

I wish she could have joined us 42 years later for our Paranormal Witness episode. We contacted her and were shocked that she not only remembered the event, but that she said it was one that she will never forget. Knowing that she went on to anchor national news and likely had covered thousands of various reports, it made us feel that our experience had made quite an impression. Unfortunately, she was touring and promoting her own book, "News Lady."

Joseph suspected that only clergy might be capable of removing whatever it was in the 'dark' room. Only years later would he confide that whatever was there made him fearful. The next visit we had was from both Joseph DeLouise and Rev. Derl-Davis. They explained in detail that they were going to attempt an exorcism. Rev. Derl-Davis was a large man with a kind face and a deep voice, with an English accent. We would have guessed them both to be approaching 40. They set the date for the exorcism, but also wanted the building empty the night before, for some unexplained reason. They wanted all of us and the pets gone for at least a few hours. We agreed, but we both began to get the feeling that this was far more serious than we imagined.

What we know today and we did not know at the time, was on that evening they were going to attempt to confront and remove whatever was in the 'dark' room. Because of Ed's attitude, they began counseling him on changing his behavior. Instead of Ed antagonizing and communicating, they wanted him to be compassionate, as these spirits are trapped and in need of prayer, not anger. I saw Ed's eyes get bigger when they explained that these things can cause real physical damage, and they wanted no one to get hurt.

Today we know that this duo could never have been successful, as both their philosophies drastically differed. Joseph intended to act as a medium, and open his mind to communicate with these spirits. This conflicts with a true exorcist, who, under no means, opens his mind and entertains communication, except prayer. So they were doomed to fail from the beginning, but we never knew of this conflict and instead, we felt optimistic. As far as we knew, it appeared that they had worked together many times, when actually this was the first...and last!

It was that very night that Dave and Ellen would awake to a ban-shee-like wailing coming directly from their living room. Dave, sleeping on the couch, awoke with a start, wondering who and what it was. The sound seemed to surround him, yet he could not see a source. It was so loud, he imagined we could possibly hear it, but we did not. Suddenly, it stopped as quickly as it began, leaving Dave to sit up and not return to sleep. He had never heard anything like it before, and from his estimation, it was almost inhuman. Ellen also heard it and immediately went and got the baby. The screams were something Dave never wished to hear again. But, as usual, Ed and I had no clue this ever happened.

The next evening, Joseph and the Rev. Derl-Davis showed up and were in a serious mood. We took Christine and the cat and left the house. Dave and Ellen also took their baby and left. We had no idea of what they were going to do, and only hoped the results would be good. It was about three hours later when we returned and found them both sitting at our kitchen table. It was easy to determine they were not happy and in fact, appeared exhausted. It was never fully discussed, but it is our opinion that they confronted whatever was in the 'dark' room and failed to remove it. There was a discussion about limiting the attendees the next day, as they were concerned for everyone's safety.

In retrospect, apparently they knew that whatever the dominate force was that they failed to remove, was powerful. I remember Ed asking what they thought the risk was, and they responded that objects might be propelled and someone might get hurt. I think it was that moment that Ed began to realize that this was no longer an inconvenience and aggravation, but also possibly a threatening situation. They were not referring to simple propelled objects, but object being propelled at a person with the intent to harm.

We went to bed under the false impression that they had accomplished something that night, instead of recognizing their failure, which was obvious in their defeated appearance. We were looking forward to the exorcism, which would be the final ritual and hopefully, the end of our problems.

Dave and Ellen significantly down played the activity in their apartment when talking with Joseph and the Rev. Derl-Davis. Ellen kept her experiences personal for the most part, and Dave knew that no one might understand his and be able to interpret them according to his native beliefs. Dave also thought the exorcism strange, because in his native beliefs, only people could be exorcised and never a building or structure. Dave was already planning to move out, but would keep it to himself for now, hoping this ritual might be successful. Out of pure curiosity would he attend, but his honest opinion was that he found the concept humorous.

The day of the exorcism was one of hope for Ed and I. Ed took the day off from work and Christine and Kitty went to his mother's. Dave and Ellen did the same. The whole neighborhood must have been aware that something was happening, as the huge NBC trucks arrived, along with a parade of cars filled with NBC executives wanting to view the ritual and possibly see a ghost. As they piled into our apartment, the atmosphere became carnival-like. For all of us that lived here, it was aggravating as we watched the giggles and laughter. This was true of everyone from NBC except Carole Simpson and her sound man, as they remained serious. Ed was steaming and I could tell he was on the verge of kicking them all out.

There they stood about 6-7 executives in suits, pointing and giggling like little children. Carole was clearly upset, but remained professional. I wondered why they were even here. Maybe they thought they might see the boogeyman, but we soon found out that none of them were brave enough to meet him if they did.

I was a nervous wreck, and was so happy when Ellen arrived. Carole Simpson was a very prominent reporter and it made me nervous just speaking with her. In retrospect, Carole was taking a huge risk doing this piece, as she was well known for her high standards in journalism and our story was a first and certainly well off the grid. She took the likely risk of being held up to ridicule should this turn out as a non-event. I wondered if that was why the suits were there if only to witness her possible failure, because it was obvious NBC put a lot of resources into this piece.

Then, Joseph and Rev. Derl-Davis arrived. As the carnival buzz continued, Rev. Davis setup a table as an altar, put candles into place and, finally, centered his bible. His voice immediately silenced the room as he announced;

"This house will be sealed. Anyone that stays for this exorcism will not be able to leave until this ceremony concludes."

There were no if, ands, or buts in his words. He was stating a fact and letting everyone know there would be no exceptions. He focused his stare on the giggling suits.

I swear, every single executive stopped smiling and one by one, quickly left the house. The problem became that the sound man also wanted to leave. We had to provide him with a cross and a bible before he considered staying. In the end, all the cars left and only Carole, the sound man, and cameraman remained. Dave and Ellen joined us, and after all doors and windows were closed, Rev. Davis began with a prayer. Joseph sat silent, in what appeared as deep concentration.

You must imagine us as we sat, not knowing what to expect. Would a ghost appear? Would things fly around the room? We all stayed sitting close and constantly making eye contact, hoping to receive any look of confidence from each other...but there were none. If everyone told the truth, we were all frightened, thinking of the possibilities of what could occur. Fortunately, this was years before Hollywood would create all these horrific images, so we had only our blank imaginations to fuel our anxiety...thank goodness.

Ed had borrowed a Sony reel-to-reel tape recorder, and asked whether he could record the sounds of the event. Strange, but we never listened to that tape until 40 years later and the 3 1/2 hours of tape did contain some surprises.

Then it began. Joseph attempted to call out a spirit, and was sweating profusely. This also started a mental and verbal tug of war between Joseph and the Rev. Derl-Davis, as every time the Rev. thought Joseph was becoming mentally vulnerable, he would call out, "Come back Joseph! Come back!" It was obvious that he was trying to break Joseph's concentration.

It became very tense as Joseph stayed under a trance-like state with Rev. Derl-Davis sweating and looking concerned. At times, Joseph looked as if he was actually in pain. It was soon that all of us could feel a presence. It was as if something was in the room that we could not see. We all moved a bit closer together. I noticed the sound man, who was wearing headphones, wince a number of times, as if he had heard something unusual. His wide-eyed look and facial expressions told the story. I wondered what he was hearing?

At one point it was obvious that Joseph had opened up to the spirit of the old woman. As he talked in her voice, it frightened the Rev. Derl-Davis. In the voice of an old woman, Joseph talked about a 'key,' a 'picture,' and a 'number.' Hearing this foreign voice was a moment that made us all feel as if we entered into another world. We had never experienced anything like this before and were actually unsure whether Joseph was gone! This, combined with Rev. Derl-Davis demanding that "Joseph come back!," appeared unanticipated and chaotic.

Joseph held out a crucifix and a tiny mirror. The purpose was to show the spirit that it no longer had a reflection and did not belong in this world. We experienced a number of things during the 3 ½ hours that flew by. At one point, the blinds rattled as if a burst of wind came through, but all the windows were closed. Then, there became a gathering of birds in front of the building in the huge elm tree and all were screaming at once. This made the sound man wince and try to mute the birds, but they were so overwhelming, even after the studio did their best, the sound of birds can be heard in the finished film.

When we did eventually pull out the old reel-to-reel tapes and convert them to a CD, what we heard was scary. On it were sounds that we never heard during the ritual. There were a number of loud, sharp 'knocks,' as if someone hit a door with a bat or club of some kind. The most frightening sound was that of a little girl. Mind you, we were blocks from a school on a school day, and in a second floor apartment that was closed, and yet clearly there is a child calling out, "Mama." The quality was clear, but she sounded distant, with a tone that seemed to project that she was in a large empty room or space. It gave us chills and, though it was recorded during the exorcism, it was never heard by anyone. Was this one of the children seen by Dave?

I can't properly describe the phenomena of the birds. It began with a single 'cheep' breaking the silence, and as it continued, the sound man adjusted his dials. Next came a second, then third, and the screaming multiplied into hundreds. It caused a few of us to look through the closed blinds, only to see a huge gathering in the elm tree. There were hundreds of birds all perched in that tree, staring at the house and squawking.

Being on the second floor, we could look out and see them directly. There was no uniformity of type of bird; it seemed there were crows, sparrows, and wrens, all bothered by 'something.' It was creepy. Without the modern equipment, there was no equalizer to silence those birds and even on the finished YouTube footage, they can be heard regardless of NBC's best efforts to eliminate them.

I have no idea why the ritual concluded. It was like the Rev. Derl-Davis just decided he had enough. Joseph was still in a trance-like state. Rev. Davis stood up and approached the altar. He then read a few bible passages and made a final statement that eventually upset Ed and I.

It was, "**This house is clean. This house is pure, and whatever is within these walls, comes from the individuals themselves.**"

When he made that statement, we knew it was obvious that the ceremony was ended prematurely and had failed. Both the Rev. and Joseph looked more depressed than accomplished. Ed and I looked at each other in confusion, as we both knew that we 'felt' no immediate change. They announced that they would seal the house from evil, and went about sprinkling blessed salt over every opening, including climbing the ladder to the attic.

Although there were supposed to be post ceremony interviews, other than making sure their names were spelled correctly, Rev. Derl-Davis, and Joseph were quick to leave. This was a surprise, because Joseph was to promote his book. We sat with Carole and she stayed long after all the gear was packed and NBC employees had left. I was soon comfortable talking with this celebrity and quickly, we became just two women. She became a friend and we did keep in touch for an extended period of time.

On the True Haunting YouTube video, at the 1.40-1.42 mark, you will see the slight appearance of a ghost. There is no door other than a vinyl accordion type, and we were all behind the camera. This was not seen by us at that time, and only a reader saw it and pointed it out.

When Carole left, I wanted to cry. I had all my faith in Joseph and Rev. Derl-Davis and I felt that if they couldn't get rid of these spirits, no one could. I actually anticipated more activity, as if to punish us. Ed was mostly silent, but I could tell he was disillusioned by the whole thing. Strangely, the house was quiet that night with no activity. One thing that bothered us was that since they meticulously sealed the house, if the spirits were still here, were they now trapped inside? Plus, Rev, Derl-Davis's last words; **that what bothers the individual is coming from us**...how could he have said that? This, when they knew they had failed? Yeah...we felt we were really screwed.

CHAPTER SIX

The NBC switchboard lit up like a Christmas tree

The exorcism was over and we were both depressed as we were, in effect, starting from the beginning. The people that held all of our hopes seemed to fail miserably and whether we discussed it or not, we both knew it. We went to sleep that night and I awoke with a start near 5 A.M.. It was a sound that was loud and frightening. Clearly, it was a woman crying or even screaming in anguish. Ed had his back to me and whispered,

"Are you awake? Do you hear that?"

I whispered back, "Yes, what is it?"

"I have no clue, but it's in the house," he replied.

It sounded like it was coming from our living room, but reverberating throughout the house. He still had his tape recorder set up and slowly moved toward it and pressed the 'record' switch. No sooner than he did that, it stopped. It was as if they were watching him. I ran to check out the baby, but she was fast asleep, as if she never heard it. We were now wide awake and talking about it. It truly was a cry of anguish that shook us both. Since most of the activity in the building was repetitive, we could only hope this was not the alarm we would wake up to every day.

Ed freely admits it was the one event that gave him goose bumps. Fortunately, it never happened again. Was it a spirit saying goodbye? Or, was it a spirit now sealed in and unable to leave? We will never know, but we agree it was something that even Hollywood could never duplicate. Only 40 years later did we learn that the crying and anguish we heard then closely resembled what Dave and Ellen heard in the wee hours of the morning, only days prior.

The day was normal, but the unusual thing was that I received a phone call from a manager at NBC. He explained that he had an interest in the event they filmed and asked if I thought it was successful. Since we really were not sure, and not to imply anything negative toward Joseph, I said I thought it may have worked. He went on to tell me of his haunting and that he would possibly call Joseph. He explained he had common activity such as things moving and unexplained sounds. In the end, I was very surprised to talk with the first person that admitted being bothered by a haunting. I could not help but wonder whether he was one of the 'suits' that fled the house before the exorcism. What comes next?

For a few days our phone was ringing as Carole, Joseph, and Rev. Derl-Davis were checking on us daily. It put Ed and me in a dilemma, for we cared for these people, and knowing there was nothing more they could do, what do we say? The whole thing was a failure? We decided it was best to tell Carole that all was well, as she was busy and genuinely concerned.

We knew if we told her anything else, it would burden her. So after a number of social calls, we assured her we were fine. We pretty much felt the same of Rev. Derl-Davis. Though he visited us often, we felt he did all he could. Our belief is that although prepared to confront a human vessel, he had no clue how to cleanse a house. He did spend time with Ed and they kept in touch for a few years, as Ed had interest in his calling. It always amazed Ed that men had the courage and faith to square off with a demon that might be thousands of years old and more powerful than most people can imagine. Ed was offered to observe a real exorcism, but declined.

Joseph was special. We never had to tell him, but he knew it was a failure. He visited us frequently and he and Ed became friends, so much so, they would go out for drinks and Ed even went on a radio show with Joseph. I can't say enough about this man, because he was gifted, he was kind, generous, and caring. He remained our friend until his passing.

Consequently, we learned that a true psychic cannot turn it on and off like the radio, and they can suffer a great deal, burdened by things they 'know' will happen, though sometimes not knowing where or when. Joseph was a gifted psychic and was also intuitive and empathic. Just handing him a personal item would allow him to speak volumes about the person to whom it belonged. The one thing we respected about Joseph, was that when his ability did not respond, he was quick to state, "I'm not getting anything."

There was one phone call that was a total scam. A reporter called and stated that Joseph DeLouise had asked him to record an interview for NBC. Of course, I agreed. Within hours, he was knocking at the door and appeared legitimate. He asked a few pages of questions and left after taking a picture of Ellen and me. I told Ed, and he shrugged it off, until a few months later when we found it was a lie and a distorted full page spread appeared in a tabloid along with the photo. "The Tattler," was not known for truthful reporting, so Ed and I were both steaming.

Carole Simpson called to let us know that they had so much great footage that it would run long at 6 1/2 minutes. Back in the day, this was unheard of, as the whole evening news was only 24 minutes after commercials. Even the president was not given that much time. She gave us the play date and it was only scheduled to run once on the evening news. Of course we could only watch, as there were no video recording devices in 1971. Ed was a nervous wreck as he was concerned how we would be portrayed.

The evening it played we were pleased with what we saw. We only felt bad that no promotion was done for Joseph's book. Within hours, our phone rang and it was Carole. She stated their switchboard lit up like a Christmas tree and the segment would also run on the 10 PM news. Long story short, it ran on all their segments of news for four days. We were then informed that outside of Illinois, a larger segment might be played on their new evening program, "First Tuesday." This was NBC's answer originally to compete with "60 Minutes."

We did not understand it, but there was some FCC rule that it could not play in the state of origin, because it already commanded so much air time that it had hit a limit. Ed and I never saw the extended segment, and the all the original footage was claimed to be lost in the NBC archives.

One of the benefits of doing the episode for Paranormal Witness was that they are owned by NBC, so they had full access to the NBC archives. They wanted more vintage scenes to use at the end of the episode. Despite their best efforts in searching, there was nothing to be found. It was all 'lost.' Because a ghostly image can be seen on the YouTube footage, we wanted to review the whole 16 hours of filming. We will always wonder, what else did they capture on film? We surely know that no one was looking for anything.

This began an onslaught of phone calls from all over from different media types that wanted our story. Understand that we were still suffering and paranoid about being made to look insane, so our phone quickly became delisted and we refused all media contact, be it TV, magazines, newspapers, or movie. People now say, "You could have been before the Exorcist, or Amityville!" Most honestly, we don't care. Our life turned wonderful once we finally were able to move out. We would not have done anything different. Besides, Ed would never have tolerated them making a distorted horror film based on our torment.

Zipping forward 40+ years, you can never imagine what SYFY and Paranormal Witness endured dealing with Ed trying to keep our story "real" and protecting our image. Truth be told, it was a combination of a kind and honest producer who vowed to keep it real and the power of our grandchildren who demanded they wanted their Nana and Papa on SYFY! This was actually the very first time we spoke in public for over 40 years. In the end, our episode, which became the season two, 90 minute finale, broke all their viewing records. "The Tenants."

Once the excitement died down, we realized that we were in the same position as before. Yes, we had a few concerned people giving us moral support, but that moral support did not stop the footsteps on the porch, or the voices, or things from moving about. What were we to do? What we did not know was things would only get worse before they got better.

This was the beginning of a very dark period for me. With the failure of the exorcism, we were left with nowhere to go. There were no more listings in the phone book to call and those few people, in which we could confide, had no suggestions. Although Joseph DeLouise had visited us frequently, he made no attempt to try the cleansing again. We felt he knew there was something in this building that he was incapable of dealing with, but wanted to know we were maintaining our sanity. Many times, he would call Ed and they would meet outside the building.

Joseph did ask Ed to be on the Jack Eigen radio show, which Ed agreed. We recorded it, but never listened to it until a few years ago. When Ed did the show, he was so proud of himself, as he traded quips with Eigen and his skepticism. 40 years later, he was really upset. As we played the show, with the long delays they had in 1971, they managed to cut anything Ed said that drew laughter from the live audience. Anyone that knows Ed also knows his mouth functions with no filter, and it was even more so when he was young.

It was only weeks after the exorcism that, once again, Ellen disappeared. This time, Dave told us she went to visit her father in another state. Once again, she left suddenly without a mention. With no one to keep me company, I was never so alone, and void of any hope. It would only get worse, as just days after Ellen was gone, Dave asked Ed if they could break the lease and move out early, giving Ed a written notice. As he explained, they could not stay the whole year. It was kind of a shock, because we knew little of the total activity, but suspected they feared what we were bothered with might overflow onto them. In reality, their activity possibly outweighed ours.

Being alone, Dave returned to sleeping on the couch. It became almost a routine that every few days he would awake to hear something picking at his lock. Now that he knew it was not Ed, he was sure it was a spirit. In his belief, since his interpretation was not negative, he felt no threat but still, didn't understand it. Was it a spirit trying to enter? Was it a warning of some sort? There was always the noise, which became something he simply lived with. Watching the chandelier sway back and forth became normal. Bolting and re-bolting the door to the basement became habit.

The only thing he feared was the warmth of the oven. No one was using the stove, yet the oven door would be warm to the touch. This bothered him so much that he turned off the gas valve. He was shocked when he soon found out that it didn't matter, as the door would still be warm at times, even though disconnected. Though he had no explanation, he was baffled as to what it meant. Did the spirit think she was cooking for him? He knew the only way to get Ellen to return was to find another place to live, so he began frantically searching with every spare minute he had.

Dave remained confused, as Ellen never confided in him. He had no clue as to what she had experienced, but could only imagine that if it compared to his experiences, she was likely in fear. Some 40 years later he told us of the guilt he felt, as far as moving away. He truly felt he was abandoning us. Regardless, he found another apartment. It was much further away from his work and on a very busy street, but the landlord accepted them having a child. Dave falsely believed that this was the answer to repairing his marriage.

What Dave did not know, nor did we, was that his marriage was already over. Just as Ellen left him in that summer, she would leave him again. He may have realized it when she returned from her father's, as he sensed a distance that he could not overcome.

When she returned, she did make it routine to have coffee with me. Today, it baffles me that there was no talk of anything bothering her, including the fact that their marriage was over and she likely already had plans on leaving Dave for good. Although I could see sadness in her eyes, she held up with a false smile, even though her world was crumbling. She left me on the most positive of terms. I had the impression we would be in touch and remain friends.

As far as Ed and I knew, they moved out and lived happily ever after; when in reality, Ellen left Dave, they immediately separated, divorced, and mysteriously she, along with her their child, disappeared. When we did the Paranormal Witness filming, it was a very depressed Dave that admitted he had not seen Ellen or his first born in over 35 years. I felt so sad when he uttered the words, "That building ruined my life." What made his confusion sad was that it seemed he had no clue as to how it ruined his life.

Just as I began to really feel alone knowing that with Dave and Ellen gone and Ed working, that the baby and I would be the only ones alive in this building during the day, I became very frightened, knowing if there was a happening, Ed could not leave work, and there would be no one downstairs for me to seek help.

Enter Ed's sister, April. Ed did not do a great job in True Haunting explaining what really happened. When April found that the apartment would soon be available, she instantly made her overture at moving in. She had a number of motivations. First, was that she knew Ed would give her a bargain on the rent. Ed, to this day, believes that one should never profit from family. Second, was that her husband could walk to work since they had no car, and finally, as I would find out later, April had me pegged as someone who would babysit her boys so that she could go out and work or socialize while her husband was working.

April was a force, and wore the pants in her family. She saw her older brother as a chauvinist, so they frequently clashed. Ed initially refused to rent to her. I don't really know to this day if he did it because of our ghostly circumstances, or that he did not want to see his sister every day. April shrewdly appealed to their mother, knowing Ed would never turn his mother down. When Ed's mom asked him to help his sister out, Ed could only agree. So instead of us earning $100 a month, we only charged her what we needed to make the house payment, which was $50 or $60. So, April and her family were ecstatic that they had cheap rent and her husband no longer had to travel the bus to get to work.

What we were totally unaware of was that April had become sort of a "flower child." Her husband was a big Irishman that was a hard worker and a good provider, but led a life with blinders on, relative to April's behavior. He let her live her life without boundaries, so April pretty much did what she liked with no compromise.

Now, this is slightly off track and biographical, but Ed never had a sibling relationship within his family. His father died young and for a decade, he was the father figure and worked to help support his younger brother and sister. So, he was always quick to give orders and speak his opinion and scold them, if need be. He loved his 'little' sister, but was not involved in how she ran her adult life, only things that overflowed onto his, or the rest of the family…then he became very outspoken.

Despite not having a close relationship with April, I was relieved that I would have someone else living in the building. In all of the aftermath of what was happening, Ed decided he only had one alternative, and that was to get a second job. Computers were beginning to take hold with more companies buying them, so the demand for programmers began increasing. He had a good relationship with the dominate force in the industry, which was IBM Corp., and within a week, they recommended Ed to a company that needed programming and Ed accepted the job.

So now he would work from 7 AM until 5 PM, then drive across the city to the suburb of Niles and work 6 PM until 10:30 PM. He would eat his dinner in the car between jobs and eventually return home after 11 PM. Then it was up at 5 AM and do it all again. His goal became saving enough money to get us out of the building, one way or another. In True Haunting, he never mentioned that he eventually added a third job, working weekends. Although he would be leaving me alone, what other solution was there?

The one thing he did do, which cost us a week's pay, was move the phone. We felt if he was gone for so many hours of the day, we could not afford a situation where we could not communicate. Our decision was moving it to the kitchen, near the door on the back wall. We also exchanged it for a heavy wall phone. If it came off the hook, I would see it and hear it as it fell. As it turned out, much like Ed replacing the drain plug, exchanging and relocating the phone ended the problem. Apparently, the previous location must have violated one of the spirits territories. Or, they just didn't like phones?

I was hurt that after Ellen and Dave had left, that I never heard from Ellen again. I truly thought we had become friends and for a time, I waited for a phone call that never came. April moved in, having seen the NBC news piece, and was excited at the fact that she possibly 'owned' a ghost. Like 99% of the population, she believed that ghosts didn't exist, or that they were more of a subject of entertainment. The only drawback was that Ed addressed her as a father would a child, which sometimes created friction and a bit of resentment.

This was probably what added fuel to April's behavior. Ed was now handling this haunting much differently, having taken the advice of Joseph and Rev. Derl-Davis seriously. So, telling April not to address anything or agitate anything and to never attempt communication, fell on deaf ears.

I could see that "you're not going to tell me what to do," look instantly. Immediate friction began.

I also adhered to Joseph's advice and even when startled, I tried to ignore whatever activity there was. I let the cabinet door remain open. If I found the broom against the door, I let it be and even sometimes, I let the mixer remain on the floor. They continued 'playing' with me by moving things around or just hiding little things. It was never a surprise to reach for my cooking spoon and find it was gone, only later to find it in the dish towel drawer. There was only one main thing that was always on my mind, and that was that I had been touched. I was always aware that I was possibly being watched. Ed never noticed that I did everything personal very quickly, and that I always left the bathroom door open.

April moved in and it was one big house party that weekend. It wasn't long before the ghosts would make everyone aware of their presence. It was that first weekend that Ed's mom and little brother stayed with April to help set up the apartment to get settled. Ed had Sunday off and we decided to go out to visit friends and just escape the building. It was after 10 PM when we returned home. We found April, her husband, and Ed's mother waiting for us with concerned expressions.

"We think someone is in your apartment."

"Why?" Ed asked.

"We were hearing things being moved around, like furniture, and there were footsteps and banging noises."

Ed raced up the stairs and entered the apartment as we all waited anxiously. He quickly returned, stating he had found nothing, but did find the green velvet chair out of place. I could tell by the expressions on their faces that they were shocked. This became a sign of what we believe was that the ghosts actually were upset if we were gone, because it happened when we were in Tulsa and would happen again and again.

It was that same night that the ghosts decided to play April's piano for the first time. It was Ed's brother, Butch, that awoke in the middle of the night to hear a single note being played over and over. In the morning, he told April and she was more or less amused and was upset that she never heard it. It was also the last night that Butch would ever stay overnight in the Campbell Street house. Because of the TV coverage, April felt like she was living in some celebrity home and welcomed any activity. This was to be a major mistake.

I began to view these ghosts as people. I associated bodies with the voices we heard and a person walking our stairs making those loud footsteps. It was like my imagination was creating images associated with each action. Obviously, I was frightened.

Even though Ed was gone most of the time, I did get unexpected relief. April began using me as a babysitter, dropping her two boys off usually mid-morning. She would normally return late afternoon, taking them back downstairs. One was about four and the other was about two. The two year old enjoyed himself playing with our daughter, and I took it upon myself to begin teaching the older one to count and to read. This allowed me to focus on the children and ignore much of what was taking place around me. Though April likely thought she had found a free babysitter, instead she was providing me with an escape. To answer the obvious, never was any activity aimed at the children...ever.

What we did not know was that April was spreading the word that she lived in the haunted house that was on TV. She soon amassed a circle of friends wanting to have a ghostly experience. It did not take her long to begin asking me to watch the children in the evening and for her and her husband to entertain a group of ghost seekers. It was an age of "mind expansion," and thumbing your nose at anything conventional. April had a steady stream of people interested in the unknown, and I believe she began feeling like a celebrity herself.

Sometime after they moved in, we decided to ask her to babysit for us, and Ed took the night off so we could visit friends. It may have been an occasion, but frankly, I don't remember. We enjoyed our evening being out together and returned to pick up Christine. As we entered the apartment, there were a number of people listening to music, with candles burning and the strong smell of marijuana throughout the house. I rushed to Christine, who was in soggy diapers and most likely had never been tended to. All I could do was grab Christine and get out of there before Ed went completely berserk.

People began rushing out as Ed was screaming and threatening everyone. I had never seen him so out of control. He announced that if he ever found pot in his building they would be gone. I was also upset that Christine likely sat for hours in a playpen, unattended, in filthy diapers. I also assumed she was given nothing to eat or drink, so I was more than upset and normally I tend to calm Ed down, but this time I didn't.

It was after this gathering that Ed asked me to keep an eye on his sister's activities. At that time, he was not so concerned about anything paranormal; only drinking and drugs. The problem was that Ed was in his own world that totally evolved around his work. On a normal work day, we talked a bit in the morning and only for a short time when he arrived home late at night. Most times he was exhausted and I knew so much of what I told him went unheard, even though he would nod his head as if he were listening. [*Husbands are good at that!*] That was the case with the first time I told him of the séances and April using the Ouija board. He muttered, "Yeah, yeah." I would later find that he never heard a damned word.

More than Ed could notice, I saw the changes in April as each stage took hold. Initially, she was up early in the morning getting her husband off to work. Typically she would be happy, as she would make her husband a nice lunch and spend time fixing her hair and doing her make-up. She would then take care of her boys. If she was going out to visit a friend, she would drop the boys off around 11 AM, before lunch, and be back between 3 and 4 to make dinner. I look back fondly on these days, as I loved those boys. Christine also loved having them around and they both enjoyed playing and making her laugh.

Despite April's independent tendencies, she was a good mother and homemaker. The boys were always well fed and clean and her husband always left for work with a good lunch under his arm. Aside from a temper flare occasionally, April was generally a happy, upbeat person. She loved her family and loved having fun.

It was only a month or so and April's habits began to change. She was sleeping later and her husband had to get himself off to work and make his own lunch. [*In those days he carried a lunch pail.*] At first, I thought it to be a phase she was going through, but it only became worse. We never heard any arguments, so it seemed as though her husband just accepted it without question.

In respect for the dead, I am going to try only to detail the various phases of what may have been a demonic oppression and in the end, possession. I am omitting many details and events, and I'm using only examples that can help people understand how these things gradually take hold and slowly drag you down into a state that can possess and control one's life. In the end, April met a sad death, resulting in being an unclaimed body in the Cook County morgue of Chicago.

Her attraction and participation with the unknown, combined with her interaction and obsession with our ghosts, was not healthy. I found out from Joseph DeLouise, that April was actually calling him, not to rid her apartment of the problem, but to ask how to open the doors and communicate. She actually wanted to know how to make the ghosts more active! Joseph called me and warned me that April was doing the exact opposite of what he would recommend and that she would only make our problems worse. Ed was always working, so Joseph relied on me to impress April that she is dabbling with something she could never control. The problem was that April regarded me as being "square," and viewed me as more of a mom than a contemporary. That, plus she was strong and commanding in her personality and resented being told what to do by anyone.

So a happy, energetic April, became less energetic and obsessed with her ghosts. She soon had one of the ghosts pressing her piano keys, and she was taking great delight in calling him/her out to perform for her friends. It was much like what Ed had done with our vibrating door. All I saw was the parade of weird friends passing through, looking for that haunting experience. Any attempt at warning her was met with hostility, as she regarded this as entertainment and loved being the center of attention.

At the time, I did recognize the changes in her personality...but only after the damage was done and I had become more educated. It was then that I was clearly able to pinpoint the various phases. The changes are gradual; first came her loss of energy, as her husband was doing the morning preparations and even dropping the boys off with me, since April began sleeping later. At the time, I thought this was because of her late night gatherings and not the result of a paranormal drain of her physical being. What became obvious was that it was not unusual for the boys to be wearing the same clothes day after day.

I began spying on April's gatherings whenever I could. I could either peek into her back window, or 'barge' in, asking to borrow a cup of sugar or an egg or something. What I saw disturbed me, for the gatherings became more frequent. In the dining room she had set up a table with candles for their séances. I never did understand her husband, who seemed oblivious to the activity. It was usually late at night after Ed was home that I would report anything I thought unusual, but normally he was exhausted and would give me the "Yeah, yeah, yeah," and go to sleep.

Soon, April was relating many things about the house and former inhabitants that surprised me. I wondered where she was getting this information from. Some of it was alarming, and I was not sure whether she was just making it up to fuel her 'ghostly' friends at gatherings, or if it had any truth. I was sure that she was not looking up any official records, as she would have had to travel to downtown to City Hall and pay fees and tolerate wait times, as all records were either manual or on microfilm.

It was an evening when I noticed she had a large group of friends over, so I peeked into her kitchen window. What I saw alarmed me. I could clearly see that they had a Ouija board on the table in the dining room. It scared me, because all the lights were turned off and the only things visible were the Ouija board, the glow of the candles, and the silhouettes of people. I knew how wrong this was, but I could do nothing about it.

That night when Ed came home, I was quick to tell him about the Ouija board. I expected an angry reaction, but instead, he just mumbled something and went to sleep. I honestly did not know whether it fell on deaf ears, or if Ed was just tired of dealing with his sister. What began as a happy family situation, transitioned into a constant clash between Ed and April. I never understood April's husband, who was quiet and kind, but removed from any emotional event.

I watched as April slowly descended into a depression. First, it was sleeping late. Then, she began not caring for her boys. Instead of a caring mom, she began regarding them as a burden on her life. I will always remember the day that her older boy began reading. I was so proud, as we had worked weeks on his alphabet and word sounds. On the day he began reading a children's book, we celebrated and he could not wait to show his mother. When April arrived, he was excited and holding the book, he proudly announced, "Look, Ma, I can read!"

Her response made me angry, and I will always remember her dismissing him, saying, "You can't read. You're too dumb."

This was one of the changes I witnessed firsthand, as her children became something she only tolerated. I know, had we not been there to babysit, she was approaching a point where she might just leave them in the apartment on their own. It seemed she no longer enjoyed watching them grow, and they had become a huge drain on her life.

Soon, her husband was making his own dinner. I didn't understand it, as she shirked her responsibilities and he just picked up the slack with no complaint. (That we ever witnessed.) When she left for the afternoon,

I never knew where she was or what she was doing, but her demeanor changed. It went from her asking politely for me to care for them, to her just opening our back door and shoving the boys in, without a word. Frankly, I was pissed at times, because there was no consideration for my time and never a 'thank you.' However, I did feel they were far better off with me than possibly being left alone.

There were a couple events that I remember well. One evening, Ed did not have to work and went downstairs to talk with April and her husband. When he walked into their kitchen, he instantly saw the boys were eating cereal for dinner and April and her husband eating steak.

He asked, "Why the hell are you feeding them cereal for dinner?" He went to the refrigerator and upon opening the door, saw a lot of food inside.

April's answer was, "They like cereal!"

Ed countered, "How would you like cereal three times a day?"

"It's none of your business!" April snapped back.

I watched Ed begin to get angry, but he walked out and no sooner than we were in our apartment, he asked me to feed the boys well when I had them. He didn't have to say that, because we were both thinking alike. He was confused, as he only occasionally saw April and from his perspective, he was witnessing dramatic changes, where I was watching a gradual slide downward.

"What the hell is wrong with her?" he asked, rhetorically.

I tried to explain what I was seeing and it appeared as depression, at which point we wondered if the marriage was going well. Sound familiar? Of course it wasn't going well, as that is what these spirits do. They attack your relationship first. Ed did speak with her husband and was assured all was fine. His opinion was that April was just going through some changes. He was surely correct, but it was not what he thought it was. Today, we would recognize that something had a hold on her and was slowly dragging her down. It had to be frustrating for these ghosts, as her husband almost refused to argue about anything, so emotional energy was rarely supplied. As April descended, he just watched in silence as she slipped into darkness.

Time slowly went by, but caring for the boys on a regular basis made the time pass a bit faster; however, I was still trapped. Ed kept a ledger and I would watch as he filled in the numbers and our debt began going down and savings began to grow slowly. His only thought was to save enough for us to escape. All the activity continued, but we ignored as much of it as we possibly could. What we did do was get a number of blessed items, but today, we know it was not enough. We should have filled that house with blessed items! I never lost my paranoia, and I lived every day as if I knew someone was watching me at every moment. I desperately wanted Ed to stay home in the evenings, but that would mean he would quit his job and we would wind up staying here much longer. I was in a catch 22; damned if I did, and damned if I didn't.

April began talking about "Henry." As far as I was concerned, the name meant nothing to me. I assumed she named her ghost, just like Ed did when addressing Ben. Once again, I went spying one evening and was given a chill. I could see the Ouija and I swear that the planchette had moved on its own. Given our circumstances, I had no doubt that this was possible, but also that it was a very bad sign. Unlike April and her friends, who thought this was the work of their invisible friend, I pictured something disturbing and sinister.

As Ed and I have come to know, if a person is able to create an opening and get a valid response from the Ouija board, it will most always be an informative or positive answer. That is exactly how you become hooked. Logically, if they responded with something frightening or horrific, no one would use them again. Ed explains it like a 'prison phone.' When the spirits line up to talk with whoever is using the Ouija, it is the biggest and darkest spirit that takes command. He will lie and attempt to gain your confidence in order to control your behavior and drain your energy. The user, on the other hand, has no idea what is on the other side and what they have invited into their life. People falsely think they can close the Ouija board, but it makes no difference if what you have invited in is already there. Some people say that the Ouija board is just a game, and to that, I say it only has one true purpose--and that is to bring something into this world that does not belong.

So, Ed comes home and this time I make sure he is listening. I told him of the Ouija board and the moving planchette. He looked at me as if I was crazy.

"She has a damned Ouija board?"

"Yes, I told you nearly a month ago."

"I never heard you...son-of-a-bitch!" Ed screamed as he rushed toward the back door and down the stairs. He began pounding on the April's back door. April opened the door and he immediately demanded, "Give it to me!"

"What?" April asked.

"That damned Ouija board!"

"Its mine!" she responded.

"I will only ask you once more. Give it to me!"

Now, I have been asked many times how to properly dispose of the Ouija board, as some people have elaborate methods for doing so, but all I can say is Ed's method seemed to work just fine. As April reluctantly produced the board, Ed grabbed it and began breaking it into little pieces.

April screamed, "That's mine!"

"Do you have any idea what this thing is capable of? Do you have any idea what this can bring into this building? I don't ever want to see one of these again!" he yelled. Ed looked her straight in the eyes. "April, if I ever even suspect you are using one of these or even bringing one into this house, I will throw you out in the street. Don't ever bring one of those things into this building!"

I could describe the ear shattering profanity filled, lengthy exchange they had, but I won't. I will just say it was loud and ugly. When she slammed the door, I thought the window would break. Ed was still talking to himself and swearing all the way up the stairs. Much like April's husband, I just stayed well out of the range of fire. Ed went to bed talking to himself.

"She has gone too far. I don't care what my mom says I will boot their asses out. How the hell can she be so damned blind? What the hell is wrong with her husband?"

I didn't understand her husband either, because the cumulative changes in April had created a whole different person. She was obsessed with the ghosts and had friends parading through that looked like people I would never invite into my home. She was sleeping sometimes past noon, and her husband was making his own lunch, dropping the boys off, and even making his own dinner. If they were hungry, it was always a bowl of cereal for any meal, regardless of time of day. The lack of house cleaning was obvious, as the dishes were always piled up in the sink.

Then began a stage we would now easily recognize today. April began not caring about her appearance. She was always one for being clean and loved wearing her make-up and fixing her hair. Slowly, those tendencies eroded. A number of times when she would barge into the kitchen to pick up the boys, I swear I could see a Myra in her, as her clothes were not clean and her hair was uncared for and she was usually making going home an angry demand. "Come on boys…let's go! Now, damn it!" I actually became afraid of her, but I kept it to myself.

What came next was abuse that began with name calling. I was glad Ed was working and did not witness this but on rare occasion, because it has always been a rule in our house that there is never to be any name calling. We never call names and never let our children call names…ever. One calls another a name, and the other calls them a name, and it escalates into things said that you cannot take back. April began a verbal onslaught of her family. She started with the boys, who became 'dummies' and even eventually called them 'retards.'

I was actually attributing much of her changes as being influenced by her seedy friends, her tendency for staying up late at night, and possibly to drinking and drugs. If her husband had any problem with it, he never showed it in any way that we observed. He basically went to work, ate dinner, and absorbed himself in one of his hobbies. I knew Ed had talked with him a few times, but it never had any effect.

It was one late night that we could hear the boys both crying and screaming. Our first impression was that we were hearing a whole new ghostly sound, but once we realized it really was them, Ed went downstairs and banged on the door. There was no answer, so he walked in. He found April's husband beating the boys with his belt, and both were crying. What he saw affected him for a long time. April was standing outside the boys bedroom screaming at her husband to beat them some more. Ed, once again, flew into a rage. Understand that Ed was an abused child, beaten by his violent alcoholic father, and has no tolerance for child abuse. He grabbed the belt from her husband's hand, raising it over his head.

"How would you like me to start beating you? I have no idea what the hell you are beating them for, but clearly they have had more than enough. I never want to hear this again, or I swear I will give you both the same beating you are giving those boys!"

As April and her husband stood silent, Ed threw the belt to the floor in disgust and walked out. All I heard was the gist of the yelling as Ed came back to bed.

"What the hell is wrong with her? She was actually giving him orders to beat those boys. It was like she was enjoying the whole thing. Is she going completely nuts?"

Poor Ed had no clue. Unfortunately, working and being away as much as he was, he never saw the subtle changes that affected her little by little. I saw it all, but not having any knowledge of how these things take effect,

I could only observe as April slid deeper and darker into another world. I never told Ed at that time, but April was scaring me. I already sensed that she was capable of violence and did not want her to focus on me or the baby. The angry exchanges with her towards her children became regular, and I was very aware that this was now her normal behavior. Ed was the only one left that she feared.

CHAPTER SEVEN

Our Guardian Angel

One evening when he took a night off from his second job, April knocked on our back door and Ed let her in. I could tell from her body language and expression that this was not going to be good, so I sat there holding my breath, as all the recent exchanges between Ed and April had been hostile.

"What do you want?" Ed asked.

"I think you're possessed," she said, with a smirk on her face.

"What the hell does that mean? Why the hell would you say something like that?" Ed was baffled. [*He also did not understand possession until we saw the movie 'The Exorcist' years later*]

"That night when you broke my Ouija board, I saw a face behind you and it was a demon's face."

"Are you fucking nuts? A demon's face? Behind me? You are whack-o."

"Well, I saw it and it was behind your right shoulder," April stated.

"My right shoulder? April, you are hallucinating or something. I think you should stop all that séance and conjuring crap. I think you are going crazy."

"I believe he is following you," she replied.

At this point, I expected all hell to break loose, but instead, she just gave what looked like a knowing smile and turned and walked out. As Ed sat back down to eat, he began telling me things that I already knew well. He thought she was losing it, and he even had a feeling that she might be unstable and possibly dangerous, so he advised me to keep my distance. I never told him all I knew, because it would just add fuel to the fire and accomplish nothing. He was thinking of evicting her, but knowing how his mother would react stopped him. No way could he throw his sister out and face his mom.

In the NBC footage is a black 'fleck' during the interview. It was one of Ed's readers that did a frame by frame study and isolated this image embedded in the film. Is this what April saw?   This is on the True Haunting YouTube video at the 1.51 minute mark. It is tough to isolate.

I was sure missing Ellen and our coffee talks, but what we did not know was that Ellen and Dave had immediately separated and were in the process of divorce. I was thinking they were both pleased and living in a much happier place. 42 years later we would learn the sad outcome. It would be soon that Ellen would take their child and completely disappear. This left Dave searching for them and in emotional pain for 35 years. As this is written, Dave has no clue where they are. On the bright side, he remarried and has a wonderful family and is a grandfather, but the thought of what happened on Campbell Street left a huge hole in his heart and his emotions are still raw over 40 years later.

My life was becoming pure hell. As I would retreat to the kitchen, I no longer looked forward to April picking up the boys in the afternoon. Sometimes she was depressed and at other times, manic, so I never knew who would walk through that door. People may read this and laugh, but my habits became almost a reflex with no emotion attached, as I became a bit angry. If the water turned on, I would just turn it off without a thought. If the mixer came off the wall, I just left it there. The only fear left was that of being touched, as I imagined a dead old lecherous ghost of a man watching my every move.

There may be some ghost hunters reading this. Know that most of our activity took place during the day and evenings. Had one entered or investigated this building at midnight, they may get some readings on their electrical equipment, but, normally, midnight to 5 AM was calm except for our dreams. It is a fact that convinces us that these ghosts function in the afterlife much in the same routines as they did in real life. Yes, they can react very negatively if you violate their domain. I think the worst part of a true haunting, is that ghosts never jump out at you. Instead, they begin a steady, subtle assault on your energy, senses, and emotion. It almost seems as though they do not want to scare you away, but would rather test your limits with a goal of domination.

It was about this time that Ed came home with another dog. She was a beautiful, gray, full sized poodle. She was perfectly trained and took to us immediately. She even took to our Kitty. What she didn't take to was the house! I have to admit that we were not thinking it through because we went out and bought a dog grooming kit and Ed spent hours making her look like a show dog. She was beautiful with a ferocious bark. The problem was that she sensed things about the apartment from the very beginning. She stayed in the kitchen with me and slept in our room at night, but she was always on edge from day one. I could tell she was seeing these things and didn't like what she was seeing. Animals can clearly see ghosts and they seem to accept it as normal unless they feel threatened.

She was threatened and displayed all the signs, with her tail down and staying close to me at all times. Within days came a bad night. Ed came home late hoping to get a few hours sleep, but no sooner than the lights went out, the poodle began growling fiercely. On went the light, with Ed showing her that nothing was there. It was there...but he couldn't see it! Eventually, all became calm and we went to sleep.

What happened the next morning was just predictable. When Ed let her out into the back yard, she took off in the same path as Holly, and jumped the back gate running full stride. She was out of sight within seconds. All I heard was a loud, "Son-of-a-bitch!" Yes, he chased the dog and we searched for her, with no success. This was the last dog we would have in this building.

April took another turn, and this time, it was no less frightening. She began telling me that she was hearing voices. The voices could be at any time, day or night. Although I was always on guard, April's energy fell to near-exhaustion. From my observance, she was hardly functioning. Her husband was doing almost everything, for if April was not in bed sleeping, she was lying in her living room staring out at nothing; not even watching TV. She had abandoned her séances and late night meetings and no longer enjoyed being in the celebrity house.

It was fall, and Ed turned on our space heaters so that they would keep the apartment warm at night. The very next morning we awoke with a chill as they were not working. Ed was confused, as both pilot lights had gone out. He attempted to light them, with no success. He climbed the ladder on the back porch and went into the attic. When he returned, he was more angry than confused.

"They turned off the damned gas valves! Son-of-a-bitch! These are just a simple lever, on and off valves, and both were set on the 'off' position."

It was this action that gave Ed major concern. He knew that even if they did this, the only gas emitted was slight and from the pilot, but the very thought that they would do this was for only one reason, which was to make us uncomfortable, it made Ed wonder what might come next. He became as desperate as I was for an escape.

There were things affecting Ed. I knew he was carrying a lot of anger but when he broke his guitar, it was solid proof that it was getting the best of him. This was an acoustic guitar that he had had since his teens, and he broke the neck completely off in a moment of rage. Unlike today where he has a collection, this was the only one he had. The music had left his life, as the next thing he did, that bothered me was getting rid of his church organ. He was always agitated, and I knew he was suffering a deep depression.

How do we get out of this mess? It seemed hopeless, as we were much in the same position as when we began. We wanted any avenue out, but we only saved a small amount of money, nothing had changed, as landlords did not want an infant or a cat. Our first intention was to find an apartment and put this building up for sale, but we were not as lucky as Dave and Ellen in finding somewhere that would accept us. So, how did we get out? Our best guess is that it was Ed's guardian angel. Yes, you read it correctly; Ed's guardian angel. It was only when writing True Haunting 30 years ago that Ed, who has a great memory, ran up against a brick wall. He found himself with a memory loss and no explanation. He interrogated me, but I also had no memory of the detail. Judge for yourself for this is what actually happened.

Ed found himself in deep despair, as he was working three jobs and we were saving all that we could, but not enough to look at high rental areas, nor purchase anything. Inexplicability, he was eating his lunch at work and found himself reading the real estate section. He came across one that stated, "Distress Sale." As he read on, it said that the owner had bought another building and his original sale had fallen through, so he was offering a building at a bargain price. So, Ed called the number.

Remember, this was early 1972 and there were no multi-lists, so you were always dealing with private real estate companies. He talked with a real estate man whose company was near where he worked. It was unusual, but the man offered to buy him lunch. They met the next day and Ed learned that this building had originally sold for $24,000, but could be had for $18,000. Quickly, Ed did the math on a 20% down conventional loan, and we did not have the $3600 down payment. So, in Ed's mind, all was lost. Instead, the man offered a solution.

He suggested Ed apply for a loan. The problem was that in the days before liberal credit terms, this seemed impossible because we had no major assets, nor did we have much equity in the Campbell Street building. The man then suggested a 'home improvement' loan. Ed laughed at this, because our building would never appraise at a value that would warrant this, since our neighborhood was actually on the way down. The bank would demand the value of the building, plus the improvement, would be under the appraised value. It was out of the question and as Ed described it, it was nice having a free lunch, but his hopes were dashed.

As he finished his meal, the man handed him a card. The card had the name of a loan officer at the Ravenswood Bank, only blocks from where Ed worked. The man paid for lunch and left Ed by saying, "He will get you your home improvement loan. When he does, come see me, and we'll look at the building."

Ed claims he was baffled. He had no hopes for a loan. Besides, borrowing a down payment for a conventional loan was actually illegal in that day. He never mentioned this, so I had no clue. The next business day, he went to the Ravenswood Bank. He asked for the specific loan officer who greeted him and offered him an application. Ed filled it out truthfully, without exaggerating. He found it strange that in a day when one had to 'beg' for credit of any kind, his application was taken with a smile. When he left, he still had no expectations whatsoever. Even at this point, I had no idea any of this was going on.

It was about three days later that he received a phone call from the bank. He was in a bit of shock, as they informed him that his application was approved and a certified check for $3600 was waiting. Ed rushed to the bank at lunch and picked up the check. He was so afraid that they had made a mistake, that he immediately took it to a teller's window and cashed it.

"How would you like the cash?" the teller asked.

"Anyway you would like," Ed replied anxiously.

The teller then took an assortment of bills, all under a hundred, and counted out the $3600. She then put it in a small canvas bag with the Ravenswood Bank label on it. Ed quickly left. He was so sure that they made a mistake in giving him the loan that he thought they might catch the error and put a stop on the check! As he puts it, he was walking on a cloud. He quickly called the real estate man and made an appointment to see the building after work that evening. He had done the math, and if we could rent three apartments, we could make ends meet on the two mortgages and the loan until the Campbell Street building was sold.

He met the real estate man and they traveled to the building. Much the same as ours, it was a two flat, with both apartments occupied by one family. The big difference was this building was in pristine condition and even within walking distance to his job. His gut was telling him that it was too good to be true. When they entered, they were greeted by the family, who were old world Italians. They were woodworkers and cabinet makers by trade, and their skills were obvious throughout the house.

The living room had a massive marble fireplace and the kitchen cabinets were all handmade. The basement was completely finished and everything was freshly painted. The family explained that it was their father that had built the house and made no secret that it was paid off and free and clear of the banks, so they had complete flexibility in accepting any fair offer. They had purchased a huge house in Wisconsin and were moving their business and family there.

The most important thing about the house was that it was clean of spirits, as Ed could feel and sense the calm atmosphere. He also saw many Catholic religious icons placed about the home. He said he just wanted to stay there! Along with the real estate man, they returned to his office. The real estate man created a contract and Ed handed him a check representing a 20% down payment. He knew that with the full 20% down, the sellers would know that the sale was guaranteed, and that they would hopefully accept the $18,000 offer.

Ed never told me a thing and I can only imagine what will power it took to keep this secret. My only feelings during this time was that I sensed something, because his anger subsided and frankly, I was not sure whether something was going on, or maybe his mind accepted our situation and he mentally had given up. It was only a day later that he was called and informed that the offer was accepted. Once again, he kept it to himself.

It was a second lunch with the real estate man and Ed was informed which bank to proceed to for the mortgage application. They had set it up for the following Saturday. Now, he could have gone alone, as my signature as a non-working mother was worthless, but he could not hold it in any longer. What he did was give me a complete surprise.

The next Saturday morning when I woke him up, he rolled over and said, "Let me sleep a few more hours."

I was shocked, as this had never happened before. Was he sick? With his recent behavior, I wondered if he was going through some changes of some sort. So I had some coffee and was puzzled, as he never missed a day of work. If he was alive, he worked. It was maybe an hour later that I heard him call my name.

"Yes?" I answered.

He replied, "You better get dressed and get the baby ready because we have to go out."

I was confused. First, he sleeps late and skips work, and now we are going out? What the hell is going on?

"Where are we going?" I asked.

His face held a big grin. "We're going to the bank. We have to sign the mortgage application for our new building."

I almost fainted. "You said our new building? How? Where did the money come from? Where was this building?" I now understood why Ed was in such a good mood, and things just rolled off his back the past few weeks.

"Damn it! Why didn't you tell me?"

"If things fell through, I didn't want you hurt. Now, it is a sure thing."

There is no way I could describe how exhilarated I felt. Could it be true? Were we really leaving this hell hole? Then I felt a tinge of fear, as I thought of the possible negative. What if the mortgage did not get approved? As we drove to the bank, Ed told me the whole story, including showing me the empty bag from the Bank of Ravenswood, which was in the glove box. With the 20% down, I knew this was really going to happen. Once at the bank, they led us into a room and with a few signatures, we were told we would know within 30 days.

This was very different from our last mortgage, as with a conventional mortgage, it was processed much faster. They set a tentative closing date a month away. I was the one that was now walking on clouds. The rest of the day was spent driving around seeing relatives and friends, and shopping modestly. This was a very happy day!

When we arrived home, we found April's husband waiting for us. It seemed that once again, our ghosts were unhappy and were making a tremendous racket. He found it so hard to believe that this noise could be so loud and defined, yet nothing in our apartment was disturbed. I began to feel like these ghosts became angry at our absence. I began to feel that they had become, somehow, attached to us, which is why to this day I worry that they may find us. Once we told Joseph DeLouise that we were moving, he was quick to advise that we take nothing that belongs to the house. His theory was that taking anything that belonged there was an invitation for them to follow. I had no desire to take a single thing.

Something Ed never told me until this year was that he knew they were attached to the building. He knew that the building was their domain. So, with a smile, he showed me the jelly jar with the bullets, a magazine from Ben's 'porn' room, and a few other items that he kept as mementos of the worst period of our lives. Truth be told, I would love for him to get rid of all these items! Yes, he kept that secret for 42 years!

Ed still laughs today at the fact that although closing was a month away, I began packing the very next day. It was all that dominated my mind. I knew soon that the dead old letch would no longer be able to watch me and follow me around or, God forbid...touch me. I had nearly forgotten what a normal life was, and I was looking forward to being normal once again. The coming weeks became easier for me to take, as I was literally counting down to closing day. Within days, Ed had the whole move planned and reserved a truck, secured some help, and had everything timed. We would actually move out, drive the truck to the closing, and proceed to our new building and move in.

When we announced that we were moving out, I thought it would bring a smile to April's face as she would no longer have Ed to deal with and would likely have parties at will. I imagined the first thing she would do was get a new Ouija board. Instead, she seemed emotionless, as if she had no feelings at all and with us leaving it meant nothing to her. It was very obvious that she was in a very deep depression. When I would see her, she had nothing much to talk about and instead of the anger that she constantly displayed, it seemed as though her energy had completely been

drained. She talked of hearing voices and openly talked of committing suicide. This 'Henry,' that was her friend and fountain of information, was
now haunting her and telling her to kill herself. When she wasn't hearing
voices when awake, she said he could enter her dreams.

Today, in my opinion, she was on the verge of complete possession
and her future behavior would confirm that. I had no idea of how to help
her. Even today, what could one do? In the future, she would be diagnosed
as manic depressant, schizophrenic, and even having epilepsy...and yes,
possession was suggested. For the moment, April had retreated from life.
Her husband defaulted to running the household and caring for the boys.
That was my only concern, as I was 'mom' to them. I watched them during
most days, I made sure they were fed properly, cleaned, and entertained.
What would happen to them after we were gone? *As a side note, it would
only be a few years later that Ed and I would attempt to adopt the children.
Unfortunately, we were not successful.*

As the weeks went by, aside from the activity and sounds that were
'normal,' we did have a second occurrence where the gas valves had been
turned off, but it was taken in stride. They knew we were leaving and they
certainly didn't like it. We did the best we could going out as much as
possible, either visiting or shopping. It was on one of these days that they
repeated one of their worst actions.

We returned home on a Sunday afternoon and, once again, there was
no Kitty to greet us. Immediately, Ed went to our bedroom and saw the
window open about a foot. He never looked out; he just ran for the porch
and down the stairs. Once again, there was Kitty, curled up directly under
the window. He picked her up and she seemed fine, except for a small
scratch on the right side of her nostril. It was Ed's opinion that it was made
by another cat, and not due to the fall. Despite Kitty being okay, I was
emotionally wrecked and hysterical. Ed went and got nails and a hammer,
and nailed the window shut.

He became very angry and unbeknownst to me he began thinking of burning the place down. He knew they could read his mind or sense his intent, and believes to this day that his thoughts somewhat settled their behavior. He never mentioned it to me, but admits thinking of it and even planning how it would be done. I tend to agree that they knew what he was thinking. I knew if they could read his mind, they knew he wanted complete revenge. I really believe that since we now had a place to go, he could have easily put a match to the place.

We then put an ad in the paper to rent our apartment. It was not as thoughtless as it was portrayed in True Haunting. We debated it. It was Ed's opinion at that time, without knowing much of anything about the first floor goings on, that he was more responsible for the activity than anyone. He felt that in aggravating them, throwing away their things and even calling them out, he created much of the phenomena. We honestly felt that without us there, the activity would all but cease.

The couple that answered our ad came to us with an all-too-familiar story. They had two children and nowhere to go. It was so bad that they were moving quite a distance from the south side. We could see the hopefulness in their eyes as they looked about our apartment. Needless to say, we accepted them as tenants almost immediately. Ray and his wife Lynn were our age and had two children. Ray and Ed hit it off, and Ed agreed to reduce the rent if Ray would care for the building. Anything that Ray could do to keep Ed from visiting there was well appreciated.

Now, there are some that say this was irresponsible, but we truly believed that it was our personal doing in making the ghost active. Joseph DeLouise thought both Ed and I to be sensitive, which would have only added to our problems. Besides that, we had no frightening images to imagine. I likely had the worst image, thinking a dirty old pervert was watching me, but Ed? He likely imagined someone with a sheet over their head at worse case, or he saw them the same as his apparitions that appeared unthreatening and human.

Remember, Hollywood had not created the horrific images of today, so in reality, a ghost did not strike fear into anyone's heart in 1971.

We hoped that the new tenants would be a change the apartment needed. Only weeks later, we would be loading the truck and moving to our new place. There is no way to describe the freedom. I would still feel apprehensive, because I was not sure whether an invisible and unexpected passenger would be traveling along with us. Ed, on the other hand, seemed to know they were house bound. I guess he was correct.

Once the truck was loaded, we proceeded to the bank. We had a surprise when we entered the closing room, as our attorney, who was a long time family attorney, was not there and instead, sent someone he knew to fill in.

"Where is Stanski?" Ed asked.

The attorney mumbled something about Stanski having personal business. The real estate man entered, along with the bank officer, and slowly, we signed our way through a pile of papers and forms. In the end, we were handed the keys. We did it! We had a new place to go! The drive there seemed to take forever, as, again, I was unwrapping a present I had never seen. We arrived there and began moving furniture in and unlike our last move, everything I set down stayed put. I walked about and felt nothing unusual. The apartment was immaculate, with fine woodwork throughout, and I loved the kitchen. The living room had triple bay windows, and was so bright and cheery. This truly felt like a home.

When we were finally finished, Ed sat back in the living room, put his feet up, and relaxed. I'm sure he felt very accomplished. Instead of the kitchen, I also gravitated to the living room and enjoyed looking out the bay windows onto the busy street. We were, in fact, across the street from a cemetery, but we could not have cared less. We celebrated by ordering a pizza. I would be a liar if I didn't admit that I was initially paranoid, and turned to investigate every strange noise and check that things stayed where they belonged. I couldn't pinpoint it at the time, but today, I know the air was lighter, the temperature was even, and there was no tension in the air. It was the best night's sleep since visiting my parents.

The next morning was like someone just flipped a switch and everything was normal. We put an ad in the paper to rent the second floor of this new building. All of a sudden, my day was bright and I enjoyed moving about this apartment and feeling comfortable in any room. I was thanking God that my nightmare was over. I no longer had to keep Christine at my side, nor was I afraid to close the bathroom door to bathe. Ed immediately quit his weekend job, and tried to quit his evening job, but the company gave him a raise to stay on and they compromised, with Ed only working a few evenings. So, Ed was home most evenings and when he was working, I felt no fear.

It is hard to explain the relief I felt, as all sensations that come with a haunting were gone. No one was watching me and my worries of being touched were gone. There were no voices or footsteps on the back porch and nothing moved! Even Kitty was relaxed, moving from room to room, deciding where her favorite spot might be. I knew it was over when I took my first nap on the living room sofa. It was the first nap in almost two years. I did maintain a bit of a knot in my stomach, and will for the rest of my life, that those spirits may decide to hunt us down someday. That is a bit of fear I have learned to live with.

We quickly put an ad in the paper and, as usual, it was only days before my phone rang. It was a sweet woman with a southern accent and guess what? Yes, they had a pre-school son and were having a hard time finding an apartment. This would work out even better than expected. She was a very sweet woman, but quick to admit she was uneducated. She mentioned in conversation that she needed a tutor for her son. It was right up my alley, because I was used to watching April's sons and teaching, so I offered immediately.

Ed met them and we quickly sealed the deal. We now had three apartments rented and could easily make all the loan payments. I worked out a deal where I would watch and tutor her son. Everything seemed too good to be true. The weeks went by with every day being brighter until we received a call from April's husband. April had disappeared.

It was actually in the middle of the night when April had left the apartment. Her husband awoke to April being gone. He wanted to know if she was with us and if she wasn't, did we have any idea where she might go. It made no sense. During these times, one could not report her as a missing person unless she was gone three full days or unless there was a sign of foul play…which there was not. I was probably the person most worried, as I had heard her talks of suicide far too often. Days later, she was found living with some cult-like people in Cicero, Illinois, and she did not intend to come home anytime soon.

Her husband, after waiting a few weeks, made a decision to take the boys and move in with his mother. He made it clear to us that the marriage was over. What proceeded was a divorce and they would split the boys, with her husband taking the older one, and April keeping the younger one. Ed and I would not see her for at least a few years.

Okay, where does the guardian angel come in? I will fast forward to 1982, and Ed was writing what would become True Haunting. It originally was intended as something to be read only by family in the future. Ed's memory is typically incredible, as he remembers numbers, names, and faces, without hesitation, but he came to me scratching his head. He wanted the manuscript to be accurate, and he was drawing blanks. It was with confusion in his eyes that he came to me and asked for help.

"Do you remember what the real estate man looked like?" he asked.

I thought about it, but as I told Ed, I only saw him at the closing and didn't remember.

"Do you remember his name?" he asked.

I had no idea, but I never worked or had lunch with him as Ed did. Ed had a worried look on his face, as if he was getting Alzheimer's or something. He sat down, mumbling.

"Marsha, I have no memory of any of the events. I had lunch with the guy, twice! I can remember the faces and names of the family who owned that building, but when I think of the real estate man, I draw a blank? I don't remember his name or anything about him. All I remember, because of the money bag, was that the money came from Ravenswood Bank. I can't even remember the loan officer's name or face? This isn't like me? I mean, I remember nothing. I can't tell you whether he was short or tall, or associate any name with him that sounds familiar."

I knew Ed never threw anything away, so he still likely had the purchase papers or closing statement.

"What about the receipts or closing statement? You must have saved that for the IRS," I suggested.

"Good thinking!"

He went for our storage boxes and picked the one for that specific year. Digging through it, the next thing I heard was, "What the hell?"

"What's wrong?"

"I have the whole mortgage record folder and the payout sheet for the closing, and it has no reference to the real estate company, or that there was even a payout, much less an agent's name. What the hell is this? I don't have a shred of memory when it comes to what he looked like, what the name of his company was, or anything?" Again, he was scratching his head.

"Just write what happened and make up a name. Not having the correct names does not negate what occurred. Don't worry about it," I offered.

That was the end of his writing for that night, as I could see that it really bothered him. As if to prove he was not losing his mind, he began bringing up the names of people that we hadn't seen in a decade and even some of his teachers at school. This actually caused a halt in whatever he was writing, because he was totally confused at this memory loss. To make matters worse, he had just taken a class on memory control, so he now could not cope with the thought that his mind was completely blank. Eventually, he recorded the events, but maintained a 'blank' when it came to the real estate company, the real estate man, the loan officer, and even what he had for lunch.

This was written as a type of diary and record, meant only for family to read, but some years later, he mentioned it to Joseph DeLouise. Joseph stated that if it were ever published, that he wanted to do the foreword. Unfortunately, he passed before True Haunting ever hit the presses. Ed had given Joseph a copy to read and he called and they discussed it. It was in one of these discussions that Ed talked about his memory loss when it came to the whole segment relative to how we were able to find a building, get the money, and escape Campbell Street.

Joseph told Ed that he believed that if a person ever meets their guardian angel, they will never have a memory of what they looked like. Knowing Ed's ability to recall, he suggested that this is what happened. Ed wanted to believe this, because it was more comforting thinking that he met his guardian angel, than losing his memory. The only problem in Ed's mind, was that this was Joseph's opinion, and there were people and a few books that told of people meeting their guardian angels and even seeing them at various times, so which was it?

Can you call on your angel and talk at will, as some people suggest, or will your memory be erased should you meet your guardian angel? It caused us a lot of research over the years, but in the end, Ed knows he was in the pit of despair when, for no logical reason, he was compelled to read the real estate section, even though he had no money to speak of. This alone was weird. From there, came free lunches, an unqualified loan, a building significantly reduced in price, and a ticket out of our tormented life. It actually sums up a miracle! How would you explain it? All this combined without any memory of the person that arranged it, is inexplicable. If you have an experience, or an opinion, Ed would sure enjoy hearing it. www.EdwinBecker.com

Everything was going well and after the first month, Ray and his wife came for a visit and delivered the rent. Although Ed suggested I never speak of the ghosts, Lynn and I did touch on the subject, as I was curious whether she had experienced anything, being home all day. She did tell me at that time that a few items had been moved, and she was glad that I brought it up. I told her of the man that died there, and that we did have certain activity. She did not seem concerned. My hopes seemed answered, as we had a wonderful evening and there was nothing unspoken.

They saw April's family move out, and Ed explained that he had an ad in the paper to rent that apartment. He asked Ray if he wouldn't mind showing it and would repay him somehow. Ray agreed, so it was a relief to Ed not having to visit that building. We spent the evening chatting and sharing what life was throwing at us. They were a loving couple, and showed no signs of any stress. They were both Catholic and very strong in their belief and faith. I was hoping that they did not visit the local pastor and ask for their apartment to be blessed, because once he would view the address, his response might not be one they would expect!

It seemed life was becoming wonderful, as Ed became very busy. Having been one of the earliest people trained on IBM's new small business computer, he was in demand as a programmer, for IBM's sales were taking off and there were few programmers to set these new machines up. He began doing contract programming in his spare time and evenings, and his wages steadily increased. All of a sudden, we could order a pizza almost whenever we wanted!

It was only weeks before I learned Ed had rented out the first floor of the Campbell Street building to a Mrs. Scott. Ed's impression of Mrs. Scott was that she appeared much like a school teacher. She was very soft spoken, prim and proper. She was a bank assistant at one of the largest banks in Chicago. He thought it strange that a single woman would want a six room apartment, but between Ed and Ray, they felt she would be a good tenant. It was also about that time that Ed decided to put the Campbell

Street building up for sale. He had not been back to the building since we had moved, and he had no desire to visit there. Enter Ron Benson.

Ed had basically called a number of real estate people attempting to decide who would sell it the quickest. Some visited us and made their pitch, but we were not impressed. It was Ron Benson that did impress us both. He was younger, had his own real estate company, and seemed to have more energy than anyone we met. He also had the gift of saying all the right things with an attractive southern accent that projected a down home honesty. He was a tall man with a never ending smile. He felt there was no way he could not sell the Campbell Street building in 30 days, given that all we wanted was the same price we bought it at. Ed set it up with Ray that Ron could tour the building so that he would know exactly what he was marketing.

Within days, he visited us and his enthusiasm had not changed one bit. However, during his visit, he casually went about looking around our apartment and asking questions. His appraisal led to something we did not expect, as he now offered to sell both buildings. We were honest with him and told him we were happy and had purchased the building only months ago for $18,000. He laughed and stated he could surely get at least $24,000, without a doubt. He was so aggressive, that he offered us something that was actually illegal in its day it was a sort of kick back. He said that when he sells the Campbell Street building, he will buy us a new stereo system, and when he sells our existing building, he would buy us the largest portable color TV on the market. This made us think.

At $24,000, we could pay off this mortgage and the $3600 loan and still make $6000 on selling this building which would allow us to move to the suburbs and buy a house with conventional loan. This would, more importantly, allow Christine to enter a much better school system. After very little thought, we agreed. We asked for some time before he began showing our new building, but we pushed to sell the Campbell Street building as soon as possible. We were on our way!

Now, this is the truth about the strange behavior of Mrs. Scott. The first month after she moved in, there was no problem, as Ray and Lynn never heard from her. They visited us and were happy, except for the small amount of activity, which was talked about with us openly. Neither of them felt any fear, nor had they had any frightening experiences. They only had small things moved about, and they did hear footsteps on the back porch; none of which bothered them. They were also not bothered by showing the apartment to possible buyers, as Ed offered them a free month's rent for doing so. It was the next month that things became tense.

When they delivered the rent the following month, they described a much different Mrs. Scott. She began complaining about the noise they made upstairs. It made us wonder if it truly was the noise, or was she hearing the thunderous sounds of furniture being thrown about? What bothered me most was that she was in the habit of voicing her complaints by popping out of her front door, and telling Ray and/or Lynn her displeasures in a nasty way. When I first heard of this, Myra came immediately to mind.

She was soon calling Ed and complaining, which didn't go over very well, as he would have rather kicked her out than received her calls. Ray swore that they were being as quiet as possible, because he worked in the garbage disposal business, and he went to bed around 9 PM, getting up at 4 AM to leave for work. They were both confused, as Mrs. Scott worked at a bank and was gone all day. In those days, banks would be closed on Wednesdays, but would be open later on Mondays and Thursdays, so they did not understand what she was complaining about. They were rarely home and awake at the same time.

I can't say enough about Ray and Lynn, as they seemed to handle everything in stride, because of the limited activity it seemed Ed was right in thinking that it was he that provoked most of the problems. He felt the ghosts resented him throwing away their things and the porn collection, and reacted to his complete disrespect. It sure sounded as if Ray and Lynn were not having anywhere near the same problems we had. It seemed the world continued to get brighter, but there was a dark cloud on the horizon.

CHAPTER EIGHT

Tap, tap; no take back!

It was soon after that Ron Benson called and wanted to show our apartment. He brought the potential buyer through and never stopped talking. We had never seen anything like it. Ron pointed out every improvement within the building and more. Plus, he knew every advantage regarding the location and access to shopping and entertainment. He left with a smile. The very next day our doorbell rang and in came Ron, waving a contract. Just as he had promised, it was for $24,500. We were living a dream, as two loans would be paid off and we could shop for a house in the suburbs, plus we could expect a new huge color TV. [A *huge color TV, which I remember as being 21 inches*] A celebration was in order. It was all smiles until Ed burst the bubble by asking, "What's up with Campbell Street?"

Ron was still wearing a smile when he answered, "It ain't selling as fast as I thought, but it will, soon enough!" He still had plenty of enthusiasm and optimism. "Remember, it only takes one buyer! I have showings lined up and it won't be long now."

So, Campbell Street was still ours to deal with. I think we both felt we had an anchor tied to our leg. Nothing would be better than to hear it was sold. We held our breath every month that our renters would stay put and that they would not have near the problems that we did. Ray, our tenant, handled everything, so Ed never had to visit the building, which suited him fine. We both knew that Campbell had a shadow hanging over it.

Here is the true story of Mrs. Scott that was not in the first book, True Haunting. First, because Ed felt it did not add anything to the book, but more importantly, was that without knowing what happened to Ellen and Dave, Ed did not see the common thread that was present within the first floor. Beginning with Myra, whatever was resident there affected Myra, Ellen, then April, and finally, Mrs. Scott. Whatever was present on that first floor took its toll on any woman that resided there...or so it seemed, and Mrs. Scott was no exception.

Ed was fielding complaints from both Mrs. Scott, who complained about Ray and Lynn making noise, and from Ray, who complained that Mrs. Scott was being unreasonable. She was even throwing her garbage on the back porch for him to clean up. It was during this period that the upstairs apartment sprung a leak in their bathroom, which Ray quickly fixed, except it created a huge crack below in Mrs. Scott's bathroom ceiling. This was an old building, and the walls and ceiling were plaster, so no wallboard could be used to fix it. Ed had the idea that he would simply buy ceiling tiles and redo the small ceiling by just covering it up.

He bought the tiles and a construction staple gun, and asked his younger brother, Butch, to give him a hand. With him on the ladder and Butch handing him the materials, Ed figured he would be in and out very quickly. He called Mrs. Scott and set up a date and time in the evening, and she approved.

What was about to happen would be a total shock.

Ed and Butch drove to Campbell Street and Ed decided to enter through the basement, as that is where the ladder was. When they approached the basement outer door, they were greeted by two ferocious dogs; a German shepherd and a Rottweiler. Both dogs were at the door growling and snarling through the window, as if ready and anxious to attack and bite. Butch immediately said, "Let's go," but Ed became angry because Mrs. Scott never asked for permission to keep dogs, especially mean ones and since Ray and Lynn had two children that could get attacked and injured. Second, was the fact that she knew he was coming and didn't tie them up or lock them in a room. Butch had decided to retreat, but Ed went to the garage and picked up a 2X4, about the size of a baseball bat.

As Butch watched, Ed walked to the basement door window and as the dogs went nuts, he waved the 2X4 at the dogs, teasing them. He then unlocked the door and literally began screaming something like, "I'm going to beat your asses!!" [*Truth be told, Ed would NEVER harm an animal*] As Butch stared in awe, the dogs turned tail and ran, with Ed chasing them. He chased them up the stairs and into the living room and ordered them to "sit!" As he did, the dogs huddled together in the corner of the room. Then, Ed realized he was standing on dirt. His jaw dropped, because exactly half the living room's oak floors were covered in about 4 inches of dirt. Both Ed and Butch could not believe their eyes.

"What the hell is this? Look at this damned floor. What the hell is going on?"

Ed did not know whether this was to accommodate the dogs from going outside, but the dirt was clean, as if someone were going to plant a garden. It made no sense. The dogs just huddled together in the corner, staring at Ed, ready to run. Ed ordered them, "Stay!"

He couldn't grasp what he was seeing. The dirt covered exactly half the room and was clean and evenly spread. Except for where the dogs had run to huddle in the corner, there were no footprints or markings of any sort.

He wondered what sense it all made? Regardless, he was angry, as he had spent hours scrubbing and polishing the old oak floors that were now covered in dirt. When did this happen? Ray never mentioned it, and neither did Ron Benson?

Butch said they then proceeded to the bathroom and within a half hour, the job was done. As they put the ladder away, Butch knew Ed was controlling his temper, but was ready to explode. He could not reason why half the room was now a dirt farm. As they were taking a final look, Butch got a knot in his stomach when they heard the front door unlock. In came Mrs. Scott with two men. One was about 30ish, and the other 50ish, according to Butch. The younger one looked at the dogs cowering and asked, "What did you do to my dogs?"

Butch knew his brother was itching to unload on anyone and found himself clenching his fists, prepared for what he thought was eminent.

Ed smiled. "Nice, friendly dogs they are. I simply told them to sit." Ed's tone was intentionally sarcastic.

The younger man looked puzzled, as the dogs remained huddled in the corner with one eye on Ed. He may have wanted to say more, but the problem was that the 2X4 was leaning against the wall in plain sight, next to Ed. The younger man glanced at the 2X4 and then back at Ed. It was the opinion of Butch that the younger man possibly realized that Ed might use it on him, so he kept quiet. Ed turned to Mrs. Scott.

"After you clean up this floor and put it back to how it was, you can pack your things and get out!"

The older man was silent and staring at the floor, but the younger man decided to give some explanation. As soon as he opened his mouth, and before he could say a thing, Ed asked in a demanding voice, "Who the hell are you?"

"I...I...I'm her nephew," he stuttered.

"Are you staying here?" Ed asked.

"Yes, plus my Dad here, also," he answered, timidly.

"Well, you, dad, Mrs. Scott, and those two dogs are gone. Pack it up. If you are not gone, I will throw you out myself and I will visit you at your work, Mrs. Scott, with the police and file destruction of property. Look at these damned floors! Why the hell would you do that? I want you out!!!"

Butch said they all stood there like misbehaved children and thought it almost funny when the younger man squatted down and called for one of the dogs named 'Thor,' because Thor was acting like a scared kitten, always keeping one eye on Ed.

Ed picked up the 2X4 and gave them one last glance. "I mean it. I want you all out of here. Consider this your 30 day notice!"

Butch had to contain his laughter, as they all stared in relief as this 6 foot, 3 inch, angry man with a 2X4 turned and left, using the interior basement door.

All the way home Butch said Ed was talking to him, but really, he was talking himself.

"What the hell is wrong with people? Two dogs and two men staying with her and I get no phone call? Nephew my ass! She is likely renting out the two bedrooms. I should have busted the 2X4 over one of their skulls. Son-of-a-bitch! Butch, don't ever become a landlord. What the hell is with the dirt on the floor? I have never seen anything like that, and I grew up in a ghetto. Son-of-a-bitch, don't even think of dealing with tenants."

That is what I heard from Ed and Butch. Butch still laughs about a ferocious dog named Thor, literally running for his life from Ed. All I knew was that it took hours for Ed to calm down. The only thing he could say was that Ron Benson better sell that place before it drives him completely crazy. What we could not anticipate was that a strange turn was coming!

In relating this event to people knowledgeable in Witchcraft, we have been told that dirt [earth] can be brought inside the home for various ceremonies.

Whether this was the case or not, we will never know, as the odds of Ed or I opening a book of Witchcraft are zero!

For me, life was normal once again, with the exception that we would be packing once more. In a strange coincidence, the company that Ed had been working for, for nearly five years, decided to sell. So he began looking for a new job. He had quite a few choices, as companies across Chicago were now planning to install computers and needed programmers. Within weeks he accepted a job for a hospital product distribution company in Northbrook, Illinois; a wealthy suburb. We found a wonderful old brick home in a neighboring suburb of Highland Park, Illinois. It was convenient to work, and had an excellent school system.

It was during our hunt for a new house that we became fully aware of our new ability. One of the homes we looked at seemed perfect. The real estate woman was confident she had found exactly what we were searching for. We entered the front hallway and walked into the living room. No sooner than we did, I felt a rather strong presence, and I stepped back. As the real estate woman tried to lead us toward the dining room and kitchen, I looked at Ed, and he was frowning and shaking his head 'no.' We both told the real estate woman 'no, thank you,' and walked out. We both felt it and knew this house had a strong spirit within its walls. Whether it was negative or not, was the question, but it was one we cared not to find the answer. The real estate woman was totally confused, as we did not explain ourselves, other than we just didn't like it. Although she pressed us for reasons that she could use as feedback, we remained vague and never mentioned the dreaded 'G' word. Yes, the home had a very strong ghostly presence.

It has been this way ever since our experience. So much so that friends have used us to check out houses that they intend to purchase. Campbell Street embedded the various physical alarms that tell us whether there are spirits present. Yes, there are the obvious physical warnings, but with us it is instant. Malevolent or benign, we instantly feel that they are there. We apologize for violating their space and we exit, and ask for God to bless them.

Christine was now talking, so I decided to return to work. I had no problem getting a job, as with the proliferation of computers also came a huge demand for data entry operators and computer operators. We did not like the day care options of that time, as they seemed more like kennels for kids, without the personal care. So we found a woman that was well known for being responsible and caring, to watch over Christine. Ed had his hands full, as he was installing the company's first computer and doing all kinds of programming evenings at various companies around Chicago and suburbs.

Every month, we would get a visit from Ray and Lynn and spend an enjoyable evening talking about our children, work, and what have you. The Campbell Street situation would always come up in conversation, but never did it seem like they were frightened or annoyed to the point of moving or complaining...yet...but we did hear that the activity was increasing. Ed had enough of dealing with tenants and decided that after Mrs. Scott moved out, he would just leave the first floor empty. It was also assumed that any potential buyer would occupy the first floor, so it might make it more appealing to leave it that way.

Poor Ron Benson. When we moved into our Highland Park house, he delivered a Panasonic color TV and was still excited about selling the Campbell Street property. But as weeks turned into months, I watched as his enthusiasm slowly disappeared and turned into total confusion. His optimism that it would be sold soon became a question as to why it wasn't selling. His smile eventually disappeared and pretty soon he was not just coming to us to report potential sales activity, but also using us for therapy, as he now needed to be told that it wasn't his fault. He had no clue.

Now the roof sort of fell in, as with Ray and Lynn's next visit came some very bad news. They had registered with the church and given the activity they were experiencing, decided to request a house blessing. The

Church shocked them when they refused to bless the house after learning the address. So Ray and Lynn decided they would move out. Ed all but pleaded with them to stay until the house was sold and giving them a financial incentive, caused them to agree...for now.

Ron Benson's visits became more and more infrequent. Then came a time when he stopped visiting us regularly, and Ed would call him to find out if there was any interest. The answer was always the same. Ed decided to visit Ron at his office and give him a full disclosure, regarding our ghosts. When he told me of his intention, I was skeptical as to whether it was the right move, for I wasn't sure it would do anything but make him think we were insane. Ed felt that at least he could supply the reason that Ron could not sell the Campbell Street building so easily, and it would also allow Ron to cancel the contract and bail, if he wanted out. We would then look for another realtor.

I knew he went for the visit and returned home very, very happy. It seemed that when Ed explained that the reason the building could not be sold was because it was haunted, Ron became excited. It turned out that both Ron and his wife were into the supernatural, and even attended arranged séances from time to time. As it was revealed, Ron wanted the building, but also wanted proof it was really haunted, to which Ed called our tenants and asked them to give Ron the full details. From what I understood, being told of things moving and footsteps on the porch was all Ron needed to hear.

He visited us and desperately wanted the building. He did bring us the promised stereo, but stated he had no money to buy the Campbell building conventionally. Ed asked if there was a way to just transfer the mortgage responsibility. He told Ron he could have our escrow account [$400] and everything in the building, lock, stock and barrel including the small amount of equity. As it turned out, Illinois had a Quit Claim Deed transfer. For $10 legal tender, one could immediately transfer property legally, which included all financial responsibilities. We agreed he could just have the building. You might think that Ron just won the lottery. *[Even though there was no lottery in 1972]* He immediately stated he would get the appropriate forms and have them at his office that next day. Seeing as his secretary was a notary, they could be witnessed and certified.

The very next day, both Ed and I took time off of work and drove into Chicago to Ron's office. Ron and his wife were both there, smiling and happy. They wanted the haunted house! I was sure he likely thought we wanted out of having the responsibility of dealing with tenants that were 30 miles away because dealing with a haunting in his mind would be fun! Within minutes it was done! We were now free of Campbell Street! They were so happy you might have thought it was Christmas, and we were relieved that the burden was finally off our shoulders. We completely forgot about collecting our $10. A copy of this transaction is included in the book, **True Haunting.**

In asking him his intentions for the building, he was not sure whether he would move in himself, or he had the idea of making it a more lucrative rental by renting it to college students from a nearby technical college. This way he could get a rent for each bedroom. We wished that all his positive dreams would come true...but we kind of knew better. People question whether what we did was ethical...but what were the alternatives? There were none. As Ed frequently explains, had we wrote "Haunted House" on the building, we likely would have gotten a fine from the city and a mandatory psychological evaluation. There were no disclosure laws in that decade, so the best we could have done was tell the realtor, who in most cases, would have laughed at us. We could not afford to leave it vacant, nor could we burn it down, which would be taking a risk that it would damage the adjacent buildings, and we would likely go to jail. So, as Ed said, "Tap, tap; no take back!"

It was a few years before Ed decided to look in on Ron Benson. What he heard from neighbors was a sad story. Apparently Ron and his wife took residence on the first floor. Ron then suffered a string of bad luck. His business

failed then his marriage and finally his health and he returned to the south-
ern state he called home.

People give us all kinds of advice at what we should have done, but
think about it realistically. No one but someone very wealthy can board-up a
house, pay the mortgage and leave it empty. We were not wealthy. The irony
is that in 1970 people would only laugh at us when claiming our building
was haunted, where today, it might be an attraction that would make it more
valuable. Go figure? If we are on radio tomorrow warning people of the dan-
gers, most investigators will pay no attention thinking they are protected or
cannot be affected. A haunting is still viewed as entertainment!

Although now free of the Campbell Street building, I found I was
not free of the emotional damage it caused me. Let there be a 'bump' in
the night, and I would have flashbacks. If I found something misplaced, I
always wondered, 'could it be?' It is now 43 years later, and I still never want
to dwell on that building. I strongly feel that they can find us. Ed, on the
other hand, just let it fall behind like a bad dream. It is like he locked it in
a room and bolted the door. He puts on a brave face, but I know he cannot
watch the remaining NBC footage all the way through. He says he feels the
air and can smell the room. I also know that 40 years later, he made them
stop the filming of his Paranormal Witness interview three different times
because his emotions surfaced.

It was only a few years later, and The Exorcist came out, and movies quickly embraced the horror genre. We never did. Every now and
then we might view a movie said to be a 'true' story, and laugh at what
Hollywood had concocted as being paranormal. What we did take seriously was to learn what it was that we experienced and what could cause
it. We remained close with Joseph DeLouise and learned as much as we
could. We also made a number of gifted friends and learned of human abilities rarely spoken of. Yes, we became paranormally educated, but quietly
so. After a few years, we could list our phone number again, knowing that
the bothersome calls about Campbell Street had stopped.

Certain things about Campbell Street never left us. It opened a door that can never be closed. Consequently, we are always very aware of spirits and there are many more than imagined. Not all are scary or malevolent; in fact, most are not. We can sense them all. Hundreds of people contacted us after reading the book, True Haunting, relating what we consider to be common activity, but don't understand it or question whether to be concerned. In most cases, our advice is to ignore the activities if they are not frightening. We have studied these things for over four decades and the answer to why they are here is still a mystery. We know for a fact that those we have encountered were once living and are now trapped in another dimension. It is a dimension that, at times, crosses into ours. Why? That is the question on all levels. How was it that I could be touched? How was it that we saw the old woman as solid as you or me? Why did we hear arguing? Why can an object be propelled or moved? These were questions 40-some years ago, and remain so today.

Unfortunately, Ed and I have not seen any expansion in the knowledge of these things. This is sad. On the fortunate side, the awareness of these things has spread into a rather large community, so we were pleased not to be faced with the ridicule that once accompanied this subject. The other wonderful thing is that many people have dedicated themselves to helping others and cleansing and blessing, sometimes putting these spirits to rest. The fact that one can get help so easily is just amazing.

The truth is that there is no one formula for solving a paranormal problem. If you can ignore the footsteps in the hall, or ignore the closet door that won't stay closed, that will work, as long as you do not try to address the spirit or feed it emotional energy. Sometimes, a blessed item placed in the room will do the job. It is always a good gesture to pray. Pray for the lost soul and that it finds peace. In more extreme cases, clergy can be of help, if they are experienced at removing these things, but beware if they are not, because they can also make things worse if they don't know what they are doing.

Sometimes, solutions are as easy, as like what Ed did by replacing the bathtub drain. In one case when we were contacted, it was a television that seemed to go on and off and suffer unexplainable interference. After a number of solutions failed, we suggested just changing the location to the other side of the room. It worked. This was much like our phone at Campbell; once we moved it to another room, our problem was solved. For whatever reason, an entity will dominate a specific place and resent having their space violated. In the interference of the television, it was communicating the only way it could, in that the television was in its space. Again, that frequent word...why?

We had a reader whose father was bedridden and was being bothered by items being moved and minor unexplainable events happening in his bedroom. A blessed rosary was hung over his bed and a blessed holy card was put between his mattress which brought it all to a halt. Why?

So many of these paranormal problems are easily solved, yet others are impossible. When discussing this with a Shaman from the Philippines, it is common in his country that with an extreme haunting, they simply burn the structure to the ground. Yet, a well respected medium stated that burning a structure to the ground will only leave the spirits wandering that ground and waiting for the next structure to be built. Which is it? There was no answer 40-some years ago, and no absolute answer today.

These spirits can affect your life in many ways and sometimes it is obvious and at others, not so much. Should one become fixed with what we term as an 'attachment,' much like Ed's sister April, the person won't notice that their loss of energy and behavior is being altered. Demonologists refer to this as oppression, as the person gradually changes their behavior and their personality becomes a world of fatigue and negatives, sinking lower and lower into a deep depression, which, at its worst, can become suicidal.

Just watch the news. A man killing his family members and committing suicide is all too common.

We get correspondence from all types. Believe it or not, there are people that not only live with these entities, but they more or less enjoy the fact that they cultivate a haunting. We know a man that lives in an active haunted house and brags about it. He welcomes investigators to come in and get whatever evidence they can. From a safe distance, Ed and I have observed the negative changes in his life; from his marriage, to his job, and finally his health, as they have all suffered. Nothing good can come of doing this.

We know multiple people that have formed rather strong attachments that follow them. Their personal relationships have deteriorated and soon after, substance becomes an outlet, as it seems wherever they go, this dark cloud follows. In almost all cases, the victim is oblivious to the fact that no matter where they move, their circumstances are always the same. They need spiritual help.

These things can be addictive, as with one woman we know, she is at times terrorized by the unpredictable activity, sounds, and visions. Yet she refuses qualified help and seems to enjoy having semi-experts and investigators parading through her home. In this extreme case, all of my recommendations have fallen on deaf ears. Eventually, I will predict a very unhappy ending.

These spirits are not to be trifled with, as in reality, you have no control. That, plus you have no true idea of what you are dealing with and the power they may wield. An evil spirit, or worse yet, a demon will never attempt to frighten you. Instead, they will seduce you by supplying whatever you may be seeking. If it is EVP's, they will bait you in a direction that will cause you to continue communicating. If it is the Ouija, they will surely give you the answers for which you are searching. BUT, who are they? Who are you inviting into your life for conversations? I see it as a paranormal form of Russian Roulette. The best thing to do is to remain spiritually clean.

I have a long list of people that dabbled in the paranormal. What Ed and I see all too often, is the result of these entities siphoning off energy. They need energy to function in our dimension. Where does this energy come from? Commonly, they will drain batteries if you enter their domain. This can be dangerous for someone with a pacemaker, or even a hearing aid. They can also play on your emotions and feed from that. However, Ed and I have witnessed far too frequently, that heart problems can become an issue. I mean, what better source of energy is there than our heart, which is the center of our body's electrical system? Yes, we know many younger people that suddenly develop heart problems.

Ed and I were very fortunate, because what we encountered did its best to get between us and separate our relationship, but somehow we hung on. People imagine that these things simply provide audible or visual entertainment, when the dangers are so far beyond what one will guard against. Ed will admit he was affected by Campbell Street, because he became short tempered and lived in constant agitation. I recognized the change in his behavior, but reasoned it was our situation wearing on him. Was it?

Know that with these things, many changes in behavior can manifest. Now, I am not referring to demons, because the list would be far too lengthy. We are amazed that in watching the local news, more people don't recognize the obvious. There are things people do that are not within even abnormal human behavior. A man does not enter a school and kill little children, without some external force driving him. A man in Maryland did not decide to cannibalize his college roommate simply because he was hungry. A father in Louisiana did not cut off his six year old son's head and put it on a stake in his front yard as punishment. I could list many more, but a common thread with those that do not commit suicide, is that they have no memory of doing these heinous acts. If so, who is in control?

Most honestly, today I look back and wonder how I survived. The only thing I can come up with is that I had no choice and was totally ignorant of how dangerous it could have become. There is a comfort knowing that ghosts are no longer a laughing matter, but I cringe at the distortions and myths created by the entertainment industry. Why? Because it does not allow the public to recognize what reality is when confronting the paranormal. The expectations are for horror and images only created by Hollywood special effects. This is why the common afflictions of being affected by these things are never recognized. Someone carrying an attachment is expected to levitate or walk on the ceiling, which is Hollywood's version.

If a person realizes that they are becoming depressed and seeks professional medical opinions, the spiritual aspect is never a consideration. Likely they will walk away with a shopping bag full of anti-depressants! Should you go to a psychiatrist or psychologist, it is more or less the same. They will probe your mind as to what in your painful childhood is coming back to haunt you. Again, you will walk away with a shopping bag full of anti-depressants. Please, never tell them that you hear or have heard voices, because you will instantly be labeled as a paranoid schizophrenic. The spiritual aspect never becomes a factor, and is most always ignored.

Faith is a powerful thing, regardless of how you worship or your denomination. Recognizing the unknown and dealing with it on a basis of faith can protect you. Understanding that these spirits, for the most part, were once people and, for whatever reason, are trapped here, can overcome the feeling of fear of the unknown. Offering compassion and prayer and not intruding into their world can make a huge difference.

Ed and I never look for the paranormal. We don't even have cable, so we don't know any of the current programs dedicated to ghost hunting or exploring haunted locations. When the book True Haunting was released, we had no idea what an EVP or EMF was. When we eventually learned, we wondered why they are using such things, because we know that strong spirits can be seen and can be heard without spending a fortune on expensive technology. We even find it humorous that millions are be spent trying to experience something that we ran from.

Although we have been invited to many venues for discussions or appearances, we avoid them. This is because we actually had our fill 43 years ago. Second, because far too many people are marketing paranormal as a form of entertainment. Don't get me wrong; I would love to see our story told on the big screen, but only if it were kept as close to truthful as possible. Ed is proud of the fact that so many people have labeled his book, True Haunting, as being educational. The only way paranormal will ever be truly understood by the masses, is if a strong amount of truthfulness accompanies these Hollywood special effects.

In the end, I think I agree with ED, but...don't tell him! His advice to those wishing to explore the world of the paranormal is...don't open that door!

CHAPTER NINE

"Should you go seeking ghosts, or touring haunted places, don't be fooled. You can falsely assume bravery facing the invisible, but remember, you are entering a paranormal zoo where none of the animals are in cages!"

Edwin F. Becker, 2015.

So, where did we go from there? Like all young couples, we strived to have the life that we planned when we met. I continued working for a number of years and, although we held interest in the paranormal, we never went looking for it. We did strike up friendships with a number of gifted people, with the most well known being Olof Jonsson, the telekinetic. Being strong believers in reincarnation took us to observing hypnotic regressions. Unlike today, where a hundred new books of a paranormal nature come out every month, we read what few there were in the 70's.

Given where we are at today, it seems obvious to us that what we experienced on Campbell Street was somehow meant to be, as it put us where we needed to be today. We thank God for the wonderful friends we have made and the opportunities to help others. Who would have ever thought we could be conversing with friends half a world away? Who would have ever thought that someone would listen to a podcast that is a month old and contact us? Our experiences have been nothing more than amazing.

Ed began writing decades ago, and did write True Haunting, more or less, as a diary and kept it in a binder for only family or very close friends to read. He has written many novels and has thrown away as many as he has published. He truly did not want to put us into the paranormal world and did ask our daughter to publish True Haunting in her name. It was our youngest daughter, Katherine that took his work and turned it into books. Although he has helped many authors, when it comes to advice on the technicalities of submitting a manuscript, he knows nothing, as to this day, he still hands Katherine a flash drive and she does the rest.

As Ed writes, I make my rosaries. Over a decade ago, he asked me if I could make one with large beads, as his arthritis became a problem. From there, it seemed all who saw it wanted one like it. This took me to the level of creativeness I have today. People use them to pray, put them in their cars, carry them for protection, and even wear them. I will create them in all configurations, whether Catholic, Lutheran, Episcopal, or other. I feel fulfilled, as each bead will create a prayer.

So many people tell us we are 'lucky.' We laugh at that, because we have jumped many hurdles that life has put in our path. I live with Fibromyalgia and I faced death when an ovarian cyst the size of a baseball ruptured in 1981. I faced death again a few years ago when double pneumonia and sepsis nearly killed me and left me with congestive heart failure. [*Ed and I have matching pacemakers*]

Ed? Forget it. One of our nephews claims Ed is made of titanium. He was electrocuted and died at age 19, before being brought back. He suffered a near fatal heart attack in 1996. He had his second heart attack in 2012 and his third in 2014. Twice in his life he was clinically dead. Today, he is recovering from what a major hospital declared as the most blood clots they have ever seen, in his left leg and is diagnosed with deep vein thrombosis.

Life has thrown a lot at us, but faith and togetherness seems to overcome, in our experience. We had our share of financial woes, as my condition caused me to stop working and after nearly 20 years on the job, Ed was downsized in favor of a person half his age, and half his salary, leaving us in a situation so many of us face, but going on 49 years...we're still standing. So when we hear the word lucky...we laugh. The best you can do is when you have jumped one of life's hurdles is thank God you made it, and prepare for the next one.

We are blessed with two daughters that have enriched our lives and are a credit to the world. We are also blessed with four granddaughters that are, sadly, no longer our babies, and are rising into adulthood. Today, rather than feeling bad about our personal health circumstances, our concern is for our grandchildren, as Ed and I have watched as our society has deteriorated to what we see today. We wonder, how much worse can it get? I mean, we feel like Bonnie and Clyde when we walk around carrying our guns for personal protection. We never saw that coming!

We almost believe that the paranormal world is an escape and a soft place to land, because the real world has become so harsh and unforgiving. Given our society, paranormal is a good drug of choice. Let's face it, what would you rather do, explore a haunted house...or a crack house! With us, it is obvious why people of all ages step into the world of virtual games and make believe worlds, because there they can hide safely from the pitfalls of reality.

The big mistake, some can make is not truly understanding that the paranormal world is a very dangerous place. When we see people offering tours through known haunted buildings, we shudder. They sell tickets like it is a carnival, and even offer snacks and lunches, ignoring the dangers, as if none exist. Those that have never met the unknown up close and personal are ignorant of the possible damage that can be caused, and they search and expect to be entertained. What is overlooked by most is that what you are searching for, is already watching you. It decides whether to perform for you...or follow you home. You will never see it coming.

I can't emphasis enough that although you are looking for 'shadow people,' or orbs, or listening for voices or recording EVP's, spirits are there and sometimes have their own agenda. The problem with going to this paranormal 'zoo,' is that the animals are not in cages. Would you walk through the zoo if all the animals were loose? Yet people walk through known haunted buildings looking for thrills. Instead, the spirits sit, waiting and watching, and can stay invisible. You will never see that attack coming. Will it be physical? Will it be emotional? The one sure thing is that you have no clue. These things are not to be trifled with, as unlike a video game, you have no controller. In fact, you have no idea what the game may be. That spirit you are asking questions of...will lie. That Ouija that answers your questions...will lie. Those spirits may or may not be who you expect them to be, and they can play you like the radio or some dumb puppy.

Although sold in this country as a toy, the Ouija board can be a dangerous object. True, it is just a board, but its purpose is to create a passage to a dimension of which we have no real knowledge or understanding. Logically, if you are able to use the Ouija and create an opening for communication, who will be communicating with you? Some dangerously ignorant people consider it to be like a cell phone, where you can dial up your uncle George. In reality, you have no idea to whom or what you are contacting. Remember, on the other side of that board is something you can't see. If there are spirits to be communicated with, it will be the strongest and maybe the worst that will take control. They will tell you whatever you like, because they want you to return, again and again, until they have command or they are invited in. Once that happens, it is too late to return this toy.

In a way, I wish the paranormal was more like what is portrayed in movies. Reason being, it would be frightening with images that would scare people away. Instead, we can fall prey to something because it simply cannot be seen. How can that be, that we don't understand the power of that dimension? We fear the Flu, but we can't see it. We fear all kinds of unseen bacteria and viruses, yet many will hunt ghosts? A malevolent spirit or demon will take you on a long suffering journey that an antibiotic will never cure. I had the cold hand of death touch me. I lived with the fact that whatever or whoever it was could be next to me and even possibly touch me at their will. No, thank you. I would much rather catch the Flu.

Marsha Becker, 2015.

Signs to Heed when house hunting

1- Varying temperatures, especially too cool.

2- The hairs on your neck or arms stand up for no reason.

3- Goose bumps.

4- A ringing in your ears.

5- A heat flash and instant agitation.

6- The air becomes 'heavy' and breathing slightly more laborious.

7- A slight breeze for no obvious reason.

8- You feel watched and possibly anxious.

9- An inappropriate scent or odor, ever so brief.

10- Just feeling out of place, and uncomfortable.

Author's Comments

Many people in the paranormal world consider Marsha and me to be sensitive or empathic. Joseph DeLouise considered this to a factor in our haunting. Maybe we are, but have lived with this from such a young age that we accept it as our normal. I am including a short story written by Marsha for another book of short nonfiction works that she contributed to. In it, you will learn some basis that may have formed our sensitivity. You will also learn why this experience never separated us and our bond remained strong. We both will admit that living on Campbell Street was the toughest years we experienced of our near 49 years of married life. That building tore Dave and Ellen apart. It then went on to destroy my sister's marriage. Finally, it ruined Ron Benson's marriage and his life. Even though our marriage was strained to the limits, we survived.

I have many emails and messages from people that have read True Haunting that visit my website and are amazed that Marsha and I are still together, for in the vast majority of paranormal cases, marriages never survive. The truth is we had something special. It is something that will endure whatever comes our way until we take our last breath. Sure we have our spats and frequently so, but we abide by the 3 'C's.' Caring, Communication and Compromise and never....ever, any name calling.....ever! We maintain strong faith, and have one secret ingredient. We've been here before!

Edwin F. Becker, 2015

WHERE OR WHEN?

My husband, Edwin F. Becker and I are both believers in reincarnation. We had many experiences that have reinforced our belief over the years, but none more compelling than the true story of how we met. I kept this story "short," but there is actually much more that could have been told. I can be reached through Ed's website, www.EdwinBecker.com.

Like all seventeen year olds of my generation, I looked forward to leaving home and being on my own. Tulsa, Oklahoma, was a clean, nearly crime-free city of 250,000, and a perfect place for a young person to get their start. My start was a bit rocky, as I was small at 4'11," and looked years younger than my age. I had no desire to pursue college, and I immediately found that living on my own was unaffordable; so I took on a roommate. I had this feeling that I was searching for something, but really didn't know what. It is a hollow, unfulfilled feeling where you are always waiting…but waiting for what? Although free of rules and liking my roommate, I still found being independent was of no great reward. I found that the jobs that were available were few. My immediate choice was to become a waitress. I bit my lip and did what I had to do, because I would be damned if I had to return home and hear, "I told you so." Working all the hours necessary for me to pay my half of the bills and have a few dollars left for spending, left me with little free time. As I celebrated my 18th birthday, I wondered; 'Is this what life is all about?'

At eighteen, one cannot see far into the future, and I searched for that undefined "thing" that I could strive to be moving toward. I knew there was something that would take me out of this mundane, repetitive existence. It was no wonder when a group of girls suggested we drive out of town to see a "fortune teller," that I agreed to go along. Today they call it "readings," but back in my day, it was fortune telling. Typically, it was assumed to be done by gypsies, but as we entered the old farmhouse, this wasn't the case. We were greeted by what appeared to be an elderly woman that, after letting us in, took her place in a rocking chair. At age eighteen, it was tough to judge an older person's age, so she could have been 40 or even 60.

She had a soft voice and had gray hair tucked back in a bun. She wore a printed dress, like you would expect a farm woman to wear, and was slightly overweight. I felt a warm feeling and almost wanted to hug her. We all sat on the floor, surrounding her rocking chair, and watched as she studied each of our faces. The other girls took turns asking her questions that one might expect of 18 year olds, but almost the entire time, she fixated on me. When, eventually, there was a pause in the questions, she looked at me and said, "Your father is in the doorway." I was in shock, for I knew she had no way of knowing my biological father had died when I was about four. Call it the power of suggestion, or an apparition that only she and I could witness, but I turned and he was there smiling, but only for a brief moment.

She then went on to describe my house, my mother, and something she really should never have known. You see, my stepfather worked for General Electric, and was chosen to use their new washer/dryer combination as a test. This appliance had not yet been advertised or released, yet this old woman mentioned it as if she wanted me to know that she was for real. Without me asking, she told me that someone would soon enter my life. She stated, "He would not be from here." Also, That I would know him instantly and I would find what I was waiting for. Although I would remember every word, what dominated my mind was the image of my father standing in the doorway...smiling.

Six hundred miles away in Chicago, a bold young man was forming a new show band. He had earned his experience working with a seasoned show band for nearly three years and was now going on his own. He was not what one would expect of a teenager that grew up working in nightclubs and bars. His initial incentive was to help financially provide for his mother and younger brother and sister, as his father had passed away at a young age. He was forming a new band, because the group he was with had decided to go to New York and something inside him told him his future was elsewhere. He was engaged to be married, but knew the engagement would not last, as he was not in love; only comfortable in his relationship. By his 20th birthday, his band was soon at the top of the groups in demand with his agency, Musical Enterprises.

They were unusual, as among the five of them they played a church organ, drums, saxophone, trumpet, valve trombone, bass, and guitar. They all sang in rare harmonies and three of them had "lead' singer voices. This five piece group, dubbed The Four Souls, began playing in venues typically reserved for larger bands. Versatility was their attraction as they could go from singing A-cappella, to the Beatles, to standards...or their signature, Rhythm and Blues. They were at home in nightclubs, supper clubs, or even college events. They appeared in suits or grunge, depending on what was expected. They were chosen to open for the Temptations when the Golden Dome stadium was built at Notre Dame University. In the music business, the more a band's popularity and demand grew, the more likely they had to travel, because the nightclubs that could afford them became fewer, so travel was a requirement of success.

He knew his musical future would be short, as he saw nothing desirable when he met "older" musicians. The majority he met had fallen victim to alcoholism or drug abuse. His true desire was to get further education, have a career of some sort, and live the American dream of a wife, two children, and a modest house with a white picket fence. He did have what he now looks back as a paranormal experience. Just before his 20th birthday, with an electric bass guitar in his hands, he grabbed a microphone that was ungrounded. He was literally electrocuted and his heart stopped. He clinically died. Only quick thinking and immediate resuscitation efforts brought him back. His recall of near death is another story. Soon after this he began having a specific and recurring dream. In it, he was holding a woman, but she was much shorter than his 6' 3" inch frame. So in the dream he hugged her and was only looking down at her light brown hair. There was nothing erotic; only this overwhelming feeling of love and security. Once he realized that this dream was becoming constant, he found himself wishing that he could see her face. Meanwhile, he continued living every young man's dream.

Back in Tulsa, I was tired of working my butt off for meager tips only to make ends meet. It was only by chance that I was told by a friend that "dancers" make more money. My background was in dance from the time I was young, only to be told that as a ballerina I could have no future, as I was too short. The dancing this girl was speaking of was in a "beer barn." In Oklahoma, the liquor laws were strange. A night club or tavern could only sell either beer or hard liquor, but not both. Obviously, the places that served beer were more working class and rowdy. I gathered my courage and went to audition at the "Beer A-Go-Go." Being nervous, I tripped on my way to the stage and in front of a beer swilling audience, an obese front man for the band announced, "Hey folks, we know she can't walk...but can she dance?"

The job was to stay at the side of the stage and dance to whatever the band played. I blocked my nerves and took my mind to a place where I could dance. When it was over, I got the job. I could now dance part time and also get paid nightly. The hours were not bad, as the beer joints closed at midnight, with the exception being Saturday when they were open until 2 AM. Tulsa was littered with beer joints, so I did see some security knowing I could always find supplemental income dancing and getting paid by the night. Life became a bit easier, but only to extent that I could now eat three times a day if I liked. Life now became waitressing, dancing, and spending what little free time with my roommate, Jan. Where was my mysterious man from somewhere else?

Ed had broken his engagement, but his fiancé and family were unhappy with his decision. He asked the agency to book him out of town, but he found that Calumet City or Milwaukee were still close enough to Chicago to be stalked or bothered by his ex-fiancé or her friends. Fed up, he asked his agency for an immediate road trip. His agent stated that with little or short notice, all he had was a big nightclub in Tulsa, Oklahoma, 600 miles away. Ed immediately agreed, though he had no idea what Tulsa was like, having never crossed the Mississippi. This was January, 1967 and they were just building the famous arch in St. Louis.

Soon, he was marveling at the sight of oil wells and the red dirt. Tulsa's finest hotel was the Alvin Plaza in the center of downtown, with a fine restaurant and room service, which is where the band checked in. Just a few blocks over was "The Fondelite," the only club in Tulsa that booked out of town entertainment. The band brought immediate attention, driving in with a new Mustang and Pontiac GTO, with their long hair and loud "Chicago" manner and speech. Ed felt free. There would be no phone calls, and no one visiting the club asking him to reconsider the engagement.

When they went to the club to set up their equipment, it created an instant buzz. They found that they were the first band ever to play this club with less than seven pieces. The employees were somewhat skeptical until the band opened their rehearsal with full horns. Word quickly spread that this little group was something to be heard. Ed prepared to enjoy three weeks in the sunshine. Their contract was for two weeks with another week's option. They had never worked a nightclub that did not exercise the option and hold them over, so he knew their stay would be the full length. It was mid-January and Chicago was having their record "Big Snow" that shut the city down for three days, but the band was enjoying 70 degree weather. None of them had ever been on this side of the Mississippi, and the friendly people and clean environment was quite a change from the surly population and old urban surroundings of Chicago.

After a very successful opening night, they had no shortage of "friends" that wanted to hang around. They were invited to parties, dinners, outings, and even other clubs. One of the girls that Ed made friends with was Jan. There was no sexual attraction, but they instantly became friends and Ed took to sitting with her on his breaks, as it was "safe" and no one would bother him. So he was always happy when Jan came to hear them, which was most every night.

Me with my roommate Jan, January 1967

Jan always talked of her roommate, Marsha, and kept insisting Ed should meet her. The problem was Jan was always inviting him to her apartment and Ed was reluctant to get involved. Word quickly spread in Tulsa, and the Fondelite was enjoying record crowds to hear this versatile Chicago band. The owner, Jerry, was a demanding fellow. One night the band played the song "Tax Man," in Beatles style. Jerry called Ed over and since he was being looked at for tax evasion, threatened Ed that if he played the song again, he would take $100 from the band's pay, so Ed struck the song from their play list. Regardless of the audience demands, "Tax Man" was out…for now. The band was enjoying their stay.

In a last ditch effort to bring Ed and me together, Jan invited the whole band over for breakfast. They all showed up…except Ed. So with Jan as the host, I met the band from Chicago, minus their leader. Jan had spoken so much about this Ed guy, that I was becoming a bit curious. The only problem in my thinking was, what would meeting a guy that was leaving town in a week or so be, but a waste of time? My 19th birthday was coming up, but it would be just another day. For the most part, I was alienated from my family, and had only a small circle of friends; most of which were distant with the exception of Jan. This was the night of my birthday. As I prepared to have a quiet evening watching TV, Jan demanded that I go out with her to the Fondelite Club. This was a hard liquor nightclub and it was also licensed as a private club. After a lot of convincing, I agreed to go just for a little while. I did not drink, so maybe I would have a coke, a dance, and come back home.

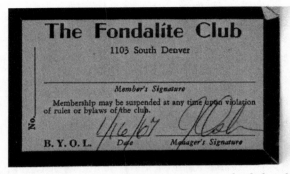

The **Fondalite Club**

1103 South Denver

Member's Signature

Membership may be suspended at any time upon violation
of rules or bylaws of the club.

B. Y. O. L.   *Date*   *Manager's Signature*

This is where it gets very strange. As we approached the club, the only thing on my mind was how brief I could stay before I exited and returned home…but as I walked through the open door, all thoughts of leaving evaporated. Jan led the way to a table directly in front of the stage. The band was on stage playing, and my eyes immediately focused on the tall bass player, who was singing with his eyes scanning the audience until they fell upon me. He gave Jan a wink and a slight wave, but refocused directly on me. For a moment, it seemed like time stopped as we made eye contact. Yes, Jan was right, they sounded amazing. Yes, Jan was right again, I wanted to meet this bass player. It seemed as they played, he never took his eyes off of me, and I did my best to project my strongest "come hither" looks. He soon announced that they would "Take ten for a coke and smoke." It was at that moment a friend asked me to dance, so I left for the dance floor. I watched as Ed headed directly to our table to talk to Jan.

I could see the exchange of words, and only later did I learn that she had told him to ask me to dance. He refused. He told Jan that although I was beautiful, I appeared to be too young. Jan tried to convince Ed it was my 19th birthday, but in a world of phony IDs he was not convinced and as I watched from the dance floor he took his coke, walked away from our table and leaned against the stage. I have no idea what came over me, but as I danced and saw him watching me from a distance, I knew I had to do something I had never done before. When the music stopped I walked directly toward him and as the Otis Redding began singing, "I've been

Loving You Too Long." I looked Ed in the eyes and asked, "Will you dance with me?" He smiled, reached out and took my hand, and we walked to the dance floor. All I can say is it was a feeling that can never be described. I knew Ed felt it, as instead of the "polite" slow dance position, he embraced me like we had been in love forever. He later told me that he knew he found the girl in his dreams.

We danced and held each other so tight that one might think we anticipated someone trying to pull us apart. There are not words to describe how we both felt. When the song ended, although it was a rule that the band never fraternized with the audience while working, it ended with Ed kissing me passionately. He whispered, "Wait for me after the club closes." He returned to the stage and summoned his band mates. Instead of a loud upbeat opening song, he smiled and counted down and sang the song, "Where or When." I knew I was on my way to a different life. As Jan sat there giving me her "I told you so," look, I just kept yearning for him to hold me again, for I never felt so safe, secure, and loved. When the club closed, Ed took me by the hand and we walked to his Mustang. I know what you are thinking, but the answer is no...instead, we went to an all night drive-in, where we talked until daylight. It was like we were both lost and finally had found each other.

He confided in me that although his band was locked into almost a year of future bookings, when they were accomplished, he was done. He had a desire to return to school and work on something called 'computers.' He later told me that he was afraid that I was only attracted to him as a musician. In the end, we realized that our visions of the future were the same. Yes, that morning we returned to his room and we sampled the Alvin Plaza Hotel's room service. It was only days later that we eloped and were married. It was the bands closing night when I learned something about this tall guy from the east. For the final song, the audience was demanding that taboo song, "Taxman." Ed looked toward the owner Jerry and then over the microphone said, "Keep the hundred bucks!" He turned and counted down as the audience applauded. The next day, we were off to Fort Walton Beach, Florida.

There is no end to this story. It is now nearly 49 years later. I have faced a number of threatening health problems and live with a congested heart. Ed has survived three major heart attacks and we both wear pacemakers. We have two great daughters and four amazing granddaughters. Life has been nothing less than an amazing adventure. Every time I think our best years are behind us, something happens that makes us both feel young again. Yes, every now and then, Ed will play the song by Otis Redding or Dion and Belmonts and...we dance!

Marsha Lee Becker   3/30/15

Author Biography

Edwin F. Becker was born in 1946, and he became a bestselling author with the release of his book True Haunting in 2011. He has appeared on SYFY's Paranormal Witness in the record breaking season two finale, "The Tenants." He has also acted as guest, host and co-host on numerous commercial and internet radio shows in the U.S., Canada, United Kingdom and Australia. He was born in Chicago, Illinois, a Baby Boomer. Coming from an abusive broken home, he spent a number of elementary years in Maryville, a Catholic children's institution. There, he learned Latin and became an altar boy. He went on to become a professional musician and spent his later teen years traveling the states with an R&B Show band. During his travels, he met and married his wife of 49 years. Entering college, he studied the emerging field of computers and eventually progressed to VP of MIS for a major health care corporation. He became president of a software company that catered to the sales and development of health care inventory management. Suffering a near fatal heart attack, he retired to the Ozarks where he opened a collectible store for a number of years. He has been writing original stories for over three decades for pure enjoyment. He has two daughters that have given him four granddaughters. His youngest daughter is involved with fostering abused children, and rescuing animals, including horses. He has a son-in-law involved in law enforcement. His life experience and interests run the gamut as he has enjoyed boating, martial arts, ballistics, comics, guitars, motorcycles, religion, and the paranormal, to name a few personal interests. Today he resides in Springfield, where he enjoys the year around activity and entertainment. He is very opinionated and many of his works contain a strong social subtext. Missouri, the "Show Me" state, seems an appropriate place to reside. His personal philosophy: "Leave everything and everyone better than you found them."